Praise for *Next Generation Leaders*

"A great book filled with actionable advice for any company looking to empower a new generation of leaders. O'Neill guides you through how to coach, manage, and lead midlevel managers to new heights, all while challenging you to be the best version of yourself."

—**Lillian I. Harris, President and CEO, Man-Machine Systems Assessment**

"O'Neill has consistently proven that leadership is not a part-time endeavor or a fad that comes and goes; it's a themed activity that involves real work, emotion, investment, vision, and a positive attitude! This text connects the dots of your future entrepreneurial success."

—**Troy Bundy, Managing Principal, Avid Technology Professionals**

"Practical and sound advice for any new leader. Our next generation leaders learned these lessons, and we have seen considerable improvements in everything from professional demeanor and effective delegation to team building and motivation of individuals. The trust between the staff and these leaders is far more effective in getting results than any of the tactics used by the generation before them."

—**Anna Gavin, President, Fireline Corporation**

"O'Neill pinpoints the formula for growing a business by cultivating leadership skills in often-overlooked middle managers, enabling the organizations to scale beyond a cult of personality into geometric growth of personnel and revenue—while maintaining quality."

—**Mark Longworth, CEO, Shevirah Inc.**

"To be successful in today's business environment, organizations need leaders that are able to operate in a world where change is constant. *Next Generation Leaders* provides the lessons required for your organization to groom leaders to work in this ever changing environment."

　　—Ray Schwemmer, cofounder, President, and CEO, CollabraSpace, Inc.

"Martin has drawn on his vast leadership experience and insight to craft a rich set of tools to help us navigate the seas of constant change. While the focus is on the development needs of middle managers to prepare for the challenges of the future, *Next Generation Leaders* will benefit all of us in developing and enhancing the core competencies we need to effectively lead change."

　　—Alan Croll, CEO, eknow, and cofounder of The Leadership Breakfast

"Martin has given both entrepreneurs and business executives an invaluable tool to aid in the development of the next generation of leaders for their organizations. Each chapter represents a stepping-stone in the journey for both existing and aspiring leaders to follow as we all endeavor to become the best leaders we can be."

　　—Leo F. Fox III, Executive Director, Helping Children Worldwide

"This book is a great tool to evaluate your leadership skills as well as the leaders around you. It is true: change does start with you."

　　—Mark Ryan, CEO, Chesapeake Mission Critical

"This book captured the essence of the culture I've worked so hard to create, and gave me a great framework to maintain that culture using the TRUST principles. An excellent practical handbook to help improve your impact as a leader, whether you're a seasoned pro or aspiring to your first leadership position."

—Jo Clarkson, UK Operations Director, The Alternative Board

"A very practical and insightful guide to grooming future leaders. Martin writes from experience as a business coach *and* a business owner. *Next Generation Leaders* is a must-read for any CEO looking to change or create a culture in today's ever-changing business world."

—Mark Cissell, President and CEO, KatzAbosch

"O'Neill provides memorable, concrete tools and a great COACH device to make us better change leaders, including how to understand and engage stakeholders, as well as guidance on how to create and articulate a higher purpose and build a passion for change. This book will be a must-read for my leadership team."

—Julie Ison Haley, CEO, Edge Solutions

"Martin combines a call for a higher purpose with tactical advice to engage and empower—whether communicating a message, managing difficult people, or developing a client base. It's a quick read but chock-a-block with helpful tools and actionable frameworks."

—Kris Kurtenbach, Founding Partner, Collaborative Communications

"O'Neill draws from his vast business experience, combined with the best thinking of other leadership gurus, to present a comprehensive approach to creating, developing, and guiding effective teams. If you want to inspire great performance in yourself and others, this is the book you've been looking for."

   —John F. Dini, award-winning author of *Hunting in a Farmer's World*

"This book will make a profound impact on how you develop your leaders. It's not just a one-time read but a user manual filled with hands-on reminders of why transformational leadership is so important and how to achieve it."

   —Rick Continelli, Partner, NorthStar Partners

"O'Neill delivers informative, sound advice for the evolving business community. A must-read for all business leaders."

   —Dave Boera, President, Marked Promotions

"*Next Generation Leaders* will have a positive influence on all leaders by giving them the tools to identify and develop tomorrow's leaders!"

   —Steve Wells, Senior Vice President, ABM Government Services

"From the COACH approach to understanding your workplace brand, Martin leads you on an exercise that ensures team development is a pillar of your culture and next generation leaders are developed to their full potential."

   —Drew Hudson, President and CEO, The Choice Inc.

"With Martin's guidance, you will learn how to identify, hire, develop, and retain the leaders of tomorrow. This book is a must-read for every CEO who's ready to start today to cultivate future success."

—**Don McDaniel, President and CEO, Sage Growth Partners**

"*Next Generation Leaders* shares an important characteristic with Jim Collins's landmark book *Good to Great*: its wisdom can be used by anyone with the desire to learn and grow and lead. The difference is that the wisdom in *Next Generation Leaders* comes from the actual successful experience of the author."

—**Paul Riecks, Principal, INSIGHT Leadership**

Next Generation Leaders

Other Books by Martin O'Neill

*Building Business Value: How to Command a
Premium Price for Your Midsized Company*

*The Power of an Internal Franchise: How Your Business
Will Prosper When Your Employees Act Like Owners*

*Act Like an Owner:
Building an Ownership Culture* (co-author)

Next Generation Leaders

Getting Tomorrow's Leaders
Ready Today

Martin O'Neill

THIRD BRIDGE PRESS

Third Bridge Press
839 Bestgate Road, #400
Annapolis, MD 21401

Quantity sales. Special discounts are available on quantity purchases by corporations, associations, and others. For details, contact the "Special Sales Department" at the address above.

Orders by US trade bookstores and wholesalers. Please contact BCH: (800) 431-1579 or visit www.bookch.com for details.

Printed in the United States of America

O'Neill, Martin F., 1959- author.
   Next generation leaders : getting tomorrow's leaders
   ready today / Martin O'Neill. -- First edition.
pages cm
Includes index.
LCCN 2016902079
ISBN 9780986253126 (hbk)
ISBN 9780986253133 (ebook)
1. Middle managers. 2. Leadership. I. Title.
HD38.24.O54 2016   658.4'3
QBI16-600038

First Edition

20 19 18 17 16   10 9 8 7 6 5 4 3 2 1

Contents

Chapter 1

One Constant:
Leaders and Change

This book is about a journey that every organization must take and every leader must know how to lead: the journey of change.

The premise is simple yet profound. Organizations that develop leaders who can deal with and lead change will prosper. Organizations that don't will eventually fade away.

Change is hard, of course. In the sixteenth-century book *The Prince*, Machiavelli, the famous philosopher, historian, and politician—and my favorite change leader—described the task of leading change as "perilous to conduct" and "uncertain in its success."[1]

And that task is exponentially tougher today, when organizations and their leaders must operate in a world where change itself—and rapid change at that—is a constant. When everything is moving so fast, standing still is a real risk, and evolving the way we think and work as leaders is a real benefit.

This book is designed to help build a new generation of leaders who understand the demands of constant change and have the tools to navigate it successfully. It's focused on the development needs of middle managers, who have so much impact on the bottom line and who are best positioned to take the reins in the future.

Whether you're looking for ways to refine your own leadership skills or you're an executive who wants to know how to develop your organization's team leaders, project managers, and program managers, you'll find the guidance you need in these pages. You'll learn to take the lead on change—however perilous or uncertain the journey might seem at first—and find your way to a prosperous future.

A WORD ABOUT CHANGE

How many times have you heard that people hate change? Let's look more closely at this common idea.

Think about a simple personal change such as losing five pounds. Do you hate the idea of being five pounds slimmer? My bet is you'd say no. If you're like most people, you embrace that idea. But you'd rather not give up the foods you like and crawl out of bed three mornings a week to meet your personal trainer. So let me stress that it's not the idea of change that people tend to dislike; it's the *transition* to the change that's the tough part.

And in an organizational setting, that transition to a new vision, that shift in a different direction, is especially difficult because you have to deal with many stakeholders and lots of moving parts.

PITFALLS ON THE ROAD TO CHANGE

Within every organization, you're likely to encounter certain pitfalls that can trip you up on the way to real change. One typical pitfall is complacency. You may believe that a change is needed—it might be due to a regulatory issue, a technological advance, or other driver—but your coworkers may not agree. You're likely to hear "We've done it this way for years" or "Hey, we're still making money." People who don't yet share your sense of urgency can slow or stop the energy for change.

The lack of a broad-based guiding coalition is another pitfall. Unless other people accept the need for change and pull in the same direction as you, change won't happen.

And that leads us to vision. People won't follow you very far if they can't see where you're headed, that is, if your vision is not well communicated. But getting the word out to the web of stakeholders within and outside your organization can be difficult. Yet another pitfall on the road to change is missing out on short-term wins. What's the best way to eat an elephant? One bite at a time. You can't be daunted by what probably feels like a massive undertaking. If that happens, you might fail to take the near-term steps to move forward, toward your long-term vision.

WELCOME TO CHANGE ON STEROIDS

The typical organizational pitfalls are only part of the challenge to leading change. As I already mentioned, change in today's world is relentless, and the sheer speed of change is unprecedented. What is happening goes far beyond anything Machiavelli could have imagined—impacting organizations and also whole industries, institutions, countries, and cultures.

Three-time Pulitzer prize–winning author Tom Friedman talks about this subject in his 2005 book *The World Is Flat*. He observes that the world has changed dramatically in a very short period of time and highlights events and trends—what he calls "world flatteners"—that have affected us in so many ways. These include the collapse of the Berlin Wall in 1989, which opened up a huge part of the world to us and ended the Cold War; the rise of "netscapers" (early adopters of the Internet); the use of offshoring, supply-chaining, and outsourcing; the development of workflow software that helps us collaborate; and the many new demands of operating in a digitized world.[2]

The point of Friedman's book is that the world is *always* changing now, and leaders, businesspeople, and organizations have to learn to cope with, manage, and even *embrace* change as the only constant.

The World Is Flat, I should note, makes no mention of social media such as Facebook, Twitter, or YouTube or other ways we communicate and work together today. Even though the book was first published in 2005, we hadn't yet felt the impact of these newer media and tools at the time it was published. Friedman, in a talk to the IBM Think Forum in September 2011, said, "When I wrote *The Word Is Flat*, Facebook didn't exist, Twitter was a sound, the cloud was in the sky, 4G was a parking space, LinkedIn was a prison, applications were something you sent to college, and for most people, Skype was a typo!"[3] It just shows you how the pace of change has ramped up over just the past decade.

John Kotter, professor emeritus at Harvard Business School and one of the world's foremost experts on leadership and change—his well-known seminal work is *Leading Change*—sees this escalating pace of change as a source of both tremendous opportunities and risks for businesses. Kotter has said—and I agree—that the key to success today is to develop competence in leading change. This goes for both organizations and individual careers.[4]

DOING MORE WITH LESS

Unfortunately, at a time when competency in leading change is an essential for business success, it's harder than ever for managers to be change agents and for businesses to retain managers and develop their leadership competencies. That's because the workplace itself, like the rest of the flatter, faster world in which it exists, is also changing rapidly.

In a 2013 Harvard Business Publishing white paper, *Danger in the Middle*, Robert McKinney, Michele McMahon, and Peter Walsh paint a picture of this new workplace. The authors focus their observations on middle managers such as program managers, marketing managers, and engineering directors—because the importance of these managers has exploded in recent years. With fewer management layers in today's organizations, middle managers are now often responsible for succeeding on projects that make or break strategic business goals. However, they must lead these projects—that is, achieve change—with fewer direct reports, less money, and less time, not to mention less job security.[5]

Turnover is rife in this middle manager segment, and those who do stay with their firms for the long haul may find themselves with few opportunities for development. For years, say the authors, firms have invested heavily in training for senior executives and new managers but relatively little for midlevel managers. And even when available, middle management development programs often miss the mark: that same Harvard Business Publishing paper showed that only 28 percent of organizations felt their development programs met the changing needs of middle managers.[6]

To reverse the trend, organizations need to support and develop middle managers so they can learn to become a new breed of leader—a change leader who knows how to connect, exercise influence, foster trust, and build commitment to a common purpose among far-flung work teams. In other words, say McKinney, McMahon, and Walsh, organizations must connect leadership development to today's real-life management challenges.[7]

THE BENEFITS OF LEADING CHANGE

Suppose your organization does develop managers who can deal with change, take the reins, and lead the way to future success. What does that success look like?

One benefit you'll see is increased productivity. Maybe you've started with what is really just a simple change, such as introducing a cloud technology or a new piece of hardware in your manufacturing processes. That's fine. It's tangible and shows that your organization accepts the fact that your customer base is demanding more from you all the time—and you have to deliver.

You'll also make and save more money. It's a natural outgrowth of increasing productivity and it's why you're in business, after all. Whether you are sitting in the C-suite, running a project in the field, or developing a product for a new customer, you have a responsibility to increase the profitability of your organization.

A third benefit is enhanced production capability. Remember the story of the goose that laid the golden egg? Sometimes in business, we have a tendency to hold on to and squeeze everything we can from that old goose—that is, work our equipment or our people so hard that barely any benefit is left. But if we're open to change, we can instead look around and find new, smarter ways to increase our production capability, which will ultimately produce significant business results.

To reap these benefits, you need to make organizational change stick. In the rest of this chapter, I provide a broad-brush picture of how that's done. In subsequent chapters, I'll fill in more details on how to lead your teams, lead your clients, and grow your business.

MAKING CHANGE STICK

Although a visionary person may see that change is needed, making change happen takes a lot more than vision. A number of years ago, our company was purchased by another company that had a visionary leader. His gift was that he could see trends in the marketplace and instinctively knew what had to be done. Unfortunately, neither he nor his team was blessed with the gift of execution. Seeing the change is important; building a company capable of implementing the change is critical. For example, you have to anticipate and address the typical pitfalls on the journey to change, step by step, if you want change to stick.

We said one pitfall is complacency. A good leader has to expect complacency and begin to create a critical sense of urgency—an emotional connection to the need for change. All the spreadsheet logic in the world won't persuade most people that change is needed. They must *feel* it.

You may have heard the story of a CEO of a manufacturing company who was analyzing longstanding purchasing practices. He found that the company was purchasing thirty different gloves from thirty different suppliers at different prices, which didn't make a whole lot of sense. So one day, he brought in thirty pairs of gloves, all with different price tags, and let them sit in a conference room for a couple of weeks, where people could see them. Those gloves helped people see how crazy the company's purchasing practice was and accept that it had to change.

Another example is from my own experience. Years ago, I managed a division that had just been acquired by Boeing, which was much bigger than my old company. Just up the street was Lockheed Martin, another huge firm, and one day I looked out my window and saw that it was hosting a fair to recruit new employees. I could see tents and balloons, and for all I knew, there could have been elephants and clowns too. The point is that it was a real extravaganza. At my company, we'd been thinking about having a simple, standard open house to recruit people. But when I saw that extravaganza, I realized we were now part of a bigger company and had to act like it. We had to think differently about how to get people excited about coming to work for us.

So accepting the need for change is the first step to making it happen.

The next step on the road to change is to create alliances. For example, if you have a team member who has influence with others on the team, get that person on board and others will follow. The gist is that you have to get many others working actively with you to make the change happen.

Vince Lombardi, the famous football coach, must have instinctually known this. Legend has it that Lombardi once coached a player named Tony who was not the sharpest crayon in the box. Lombardi used to develop each play at a level that Tony could understand. If Tony got it, it meant the whole team would get it and would execute the play.

Napoleon, the great military leader, did something similar. Folklore suggests that he had his battle memos written at a second-grade level so he could be sure all his troops understood and followed his orders. The creation of an alliance is critical.

But even with your alliance in play, you must never forget to continuously communicate a powerful vision of the change and your strategy for achieving it. Use every channel: your internal portal, social media, town hall meetings, a well-crafted elevator speech. As a leader, your job is to communicate your vision and be excited about it all the way through the process, not just at the beginning.

Here's a story that shows what I mean about communication. Bill Toler, former president of Campbell Soup Company and current CEO and president of Hostess Brands, once gave a talk at Campbells' national sales meeting about what the term "return on invested capital" meant. He felt comfortable he'd gotten his point across well. Three months later, he gave the same talk to the same sales team, but it didn't seem to go over well at all. Afterward, he asked a brave sales manager what had happened since the last speech. The problem was that not much had happened. "We only heard it once," said the manager, "so we didn't think it was that important."[8]

The lesson is this: if you are a leader and you don't go home at night sick and tired of communicating, you haven't done enough communicating.

Another crucial step to making change stick is to turn analysis into action. You may have gotten people to understand and commit to your vision, but now you have to turn that into action. Ask people to take specific steps to get them involved. It might be something as simple as taking a training class or setting up a client meeting. Action means movement, and nothing significant was ever accomplished without movement.

You must also manufacture early wins. You may even want to have one in your back pocket: plan for an early result that you know is achievable, and when it happens, tout it so you can energize your people. Think of a flywheel; that's the revolving wheel in a machine that increases the machine's momentum. If you give a flywheel enough juice at the start, it gains momentum and can provide stability or a reserve of available power during any power interruptions. Short-term wins are the juice that provides momentum and power for organizational change.

Once you're making progress, the next step is to consolidate those changes by incorporating them into the fabric of the company. When your initial round of changes has become institutionalized, part of the everyday operations of the company, then you're free to make further changes. You can't let up and allow complacency to return.

Consider this story about former secretary of state Henry Kissinger and one of his interns. The intern wrote a paper and gave it to Kissinger to read. A couple of days later, Kissinger told the intern, "I think you could do better." The intern took the paper back, worked on it some more and gave it back to Kissinger, who, after a couple of days, told the intern, "I still think you could do better." This whole process was repeated once again, and finally the intern brought the paper back to Kissinger, telling him, "This is the best it can be." Kissinger responded, "Okay, I'll read it now."[9]

The lesson is that every change is a lot of work, but even if you've done a lot, more still needs to be done. Don't sit on your laurels. Keep thinking of how you can refine the change and advance it. Every organization has a natural tendency to slide back to the status quo. Your role as a leader is to provide a backstop for organizational backsliding.

And the last step is to turn the change into processes. You've already started to build the change into the fabric of the culture. Now keep it going. Speeches and words become well-defined and accepted business processes. Brainstorming scrums become an organizational structure. Collaboration becomes a pillar of the culture. Use any communication channel, any tool, any technique you can find to make sure all your stakeholders—current team-mates, new employees, clients—know this message: "We're not going backward. This is how we work now."

And you will find that this message rings true—that you are now living the change you'd only envisioned at the start of your journey.

Chapter 2

COACH Will Help You

A coach can help bring out the best in you as a change leader, and the COACH mnemonic will help you keep in mind the tools for leading change that sticks:

- **C**ommunicating
- **O**verseeing team development
- **A**ligning business constructs
- **C**reating the next generation of leaders
- **H**aving a higher purpose

Let's review each of these tools in detail.

COMMUNICATING

I've already talked about the need to communicate at every phase of the change process. Now I want to give you some specific communication techniques—some strategic, some tactical—that will make you a more effective leader.

BE AUTHENTIC

Being authentic is about being believable. Nick Morgan's book *Trust Me* includes some ideas on being authentic.

First, you need to look comfortable with what you are saying, so if you're going to be speaking about your change initiative, practice beforehand. And even more important, you need to own the change. Even if you are communicating someone else's vision or change initiative, find a way to make it yours. You must also know how to connect with the audience. Try to get a sense of their emotional state and talk about some of *their* issues and not just yours. Be passionate. Don't just convey information; talk about why your topic is important and how you feel about it. Finally, make sure you listen. Get a sense of how people are receiving your information; for example, observe their body language and check for eye contact.[1]

UNDERSTAND YOUR STAKEHOLDERS

The list of your stakeholders can be pretty long. It can include teammates, employees, bosses, clients, customers, suppliers, and regulators—basically, any of the many parties who impact or who are impacted by your project or change initiative.

The better your communication with your stakeholders, the stronger your relationships with them are likely to be. And that helps you know more about how to deliver desired results to them and strengthens the relationships even more. It's a kind of virtuous cycle.

In *The Trusted Advisor*, David Maister, Charles Green, and Robert Galford offer a way to assess our relationships with stakeholders. The authors' focus is the crucial consultant-client relationship in professional services firms, but the approach is universal and can be applied more broadly to other stakeholder relationships, other types of companies, and even other industries. Figure 2.1 will help you visualize the stages of any consultant-client relationship.[2]

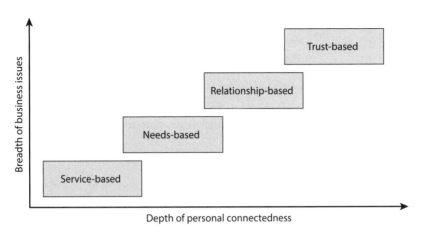

Figure 2.1 Stages of the client-consultant relationship

You'll see that the x axis measures the depth of your personal connectedness and the y axis measures your understanding of your client's business. As your personal connectedness strengthens and your knowledge of the client's business increases, you move from completing technical tasks to ultimately spending time with the client on strategic issues.

At the *service-based* level, you are providing good service, but that's it. At the *needs-based* level, you've become more of a problem solver. The *relationship-based* level is really about you and your intimacy with the client: you're consulted about what you think, which can lead to discussing new opportunities and the possibility of gaining repeat business. At the *trust-based* level, you understand the needs of the client, not just as a representative of his or her business but as an individual, and you've become someone the client turns to first for counsel, perhaps even on personal issues.

Because relationship building is so important to a leader's influence, chapter 6 will help you understand the benefits of relationships and how to evolve and maintain them with trust as the foundation. But know this now: whatever level of trust you've achieved in your relationships with stakeholders, you always have to do your best to identify and address stakeholders' individual needs for information. To scope out multiple stakeholders' needs, you can conduct a stakeholder analysis. Figure 2.2 shows how this process works.

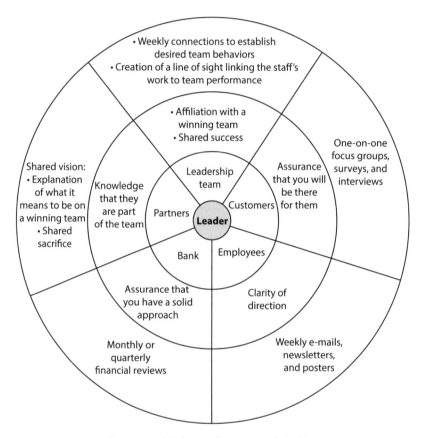

Figure 2.2 Understanding your stakeholders

Start at the center of the wheel diagram: you, as the leader, must come up with a list of your primary stakeholders. In this example, you're a project manager and you've determined that your stakeholders are your partners, the leadership team at your firm, your customers, employees, and the bank. (Whether you're leading a project, a team, or a company, the process is the same.) Next, you must think about what each of them needs from you in the way of data, assurances of success, and so on. Finally, you need to decide the best method (timing, channel, etc.) for delivering the information to them.

Notice that you do not deliver the same set of information in the same way to all stakeholders. Employees may need frequent direction and reminders via multiple channels, while the bank is fine with a single monthly or quarterly report. You must tailor communications to each stakeholder's needs.

USE EFFICIENT (EVEN UNIQUE) COMMUNICATION TOOLS

Leaders are always adding tools and techniques to their personal tool kit. A few well-conceived tools can make a substantial difference in how effectively you communicate as a leader.

One tactic is team huddles. For the life of a project, get the team together regularly for a brief informal meeting; it could be a stand-up meeting or a quick conference call. It's meant to be an intense and productive meeting where information is shared, actions are agreed upon, and deadlines are set.

Another great tool is something I call a "5-15." This is a periodic written report to the team and leadership. It should take no more than fifteen minutes to write and no more than five minutes to read. Any format—a document, an e-mail, a slide deck—will work. It's a way to keep people up to date without being a time killer.

A method a lot of leaders use to keep track of what's happening in the trenches is one-over-ones. The idea is to set up a regular meeting with your direct reports and with the people who work for your direct reports. You'll learn what's happening a couple of levels down from your ivory tower, plus it will give you an opportunity to share your vision. It will be well worth your time.

Also think about unique forums that might work in your organization's culture. In my old firm, we had "donuts with the director." People would show up and brainstorm ideas, giving the director an idea of what was going on in the company. Open your mind to the possibilities for your company. Your objective should be a constant drumbeat of pertinent and timely information that keeps the team focused on their business objectives.

OVERSEEING TEAM DEVELOPMENT

If you're a typical manager, much of the change in which you're involved is likely to be project based. You probably lead at least one project and perhaps many. So you need to understand the dynamics of project teams and how to manage and develop them.

First you need to know about the basic moving parts of project work. Figure 2.3 can help you with this.

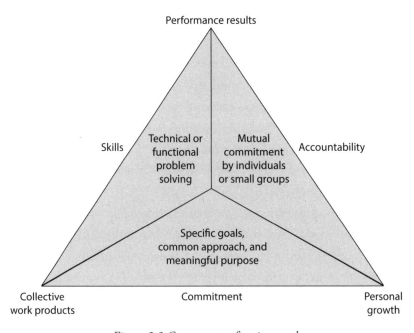

Figure 2.3 Components of project work

You'll see project work has three components—deliverables that are represented by the vertices of the triangle. Performance results (at the top) are what the client—internal or external—receives as a result of the project. Personal growth (the right vertex) is about what the people on your team get out of their work. The collective work products (the left vertex) are the specific actions and tangible products of the team's work. All three of these components are related, and you have to manage them all. For example, you don't want to produce a highly functional and expensive work product if it's not what the client wants. And the client will not get much benefit from a work product that is subpar, even though the team members may have personally grown.

So how do you get the results you need? You have to inspire commitment (the base of the triangle) among team members. Have they embraced common goals? Do they know people are relying on them? Are they committed to a common approach? Do they understand the purpose and find meaning in it?

You also have to nurture accountability (the right side of the triangle). Your team must feel a responsibility to one another and to the broader vision and purpose so they're not operating in a vacuum. Individuals or small groups of people must be mutually accountable for customer-centric results as well as personal growth.

When commitment and accountability are high, your team members are focusing all their skills (the left side of the triangle) and growing them with help from you to deliver the right work products and generate the right performance results.

You also need to know that teams tend to evolve in recognizable stages over time. You'll want to adapt your leadership style for each stage so you can keep the development process going. This fundamental concept of leadership was first presented in 1972 by Paul Hersey and Ken Blanchard in *Management of Organizational Behavior*. Subsequently, Blanchard and coauthors Donald Carew and Eunice Parisi-Carew, in their 1982 book *The One Minute Manager Builds High Performing Teams*, broke down team development into four stages.[3]

In the first stage, *orientation*, you must direct people in a way that helps them develop their skills, and you must clarify individual roles as well as team and organizational goals. However, after that stage, a period of *dissatisfaction* often kicks in; this is when you use a coaching rather than a directive style and you may need to do some conflict resolution. In the *resolution* stage, your role is to support people as they grow, as a team and as individuals, in their accountability and responsibility for outcomes. Finally, at the *production* stage, you're delegating almost completely; you mainly just monitor the team's performance against the goals.

By the fourth stage, the group has developed into a real team: a small number of people with complementary skills committed to a common purpose, performance goals, and approach who are mutually accountable and responsible for results.

The next chapter covers more about team development. But right now, let's look at some common approaches to building team performance. They're not unlike the steps to making change stick described earlier.

For instance, from the get-go, you should establish a sense of urgency and a clear direction. Identify the skills you need and assemble the right team, and be sure to set the tone and expectations for behavior with your first meetings and actions. Also, define and achieve some immediate goals and tasks, such as the deliverable of a prototype or the result of a client interview. And going forward, challenge the team regularly with fresh facts and information, and exploit the power of positive feedback, recognition, and rewards.

Additionally, spend lots of time with your team. This step is challenging because likely you'll have to do some of it virtually, but it's important. Historians have learned that in World War II, the battle in Europe was not won by the generals but by the sergeants, second lieutenants, and captains at the front. Generals rarely came to the front and some of the worst wartime disasters stemmed from the fact that they didn't know what their troops at the front knew all too well. Consistent wins amid the disasters came from small front-line groups with tight connections to their leaders.

Colonel John Boyd, the American fighter pilot who changed the way every air force in the world flies and fights and taught the United States Marines how to fight a war on the ground, gave us a key concept for small-team decision making: the OODA Loop—observe, orient, decide, and act. Boyd's OODA Loop concept is the basis for the modern conclusion that leaders have to be in close touch with their teams if they want to remain effective. The ability to decide and act based on observation and an awareness of the current situation (orientation) is fundamental to all next generation leaders.[4]

Before leaving this topic, let's review a famous example of the ultimate high-performing team: the mission control team for Apollo 13. The famous line "Houston, we have a problem," spoken by Tom Hanks's character in the movie *Apollo 13* (although astronaut Jim Lovell actually said, "Houston, we've had a problem"), reminds us of the amazing work of the team and its leader, Gene Kranz, to bring the Apollo 13 astronauts back to earth safely after an explosion on board their space capsule. Kranz operated by this rule: "Failure is not an option." Given the high stakes and the outstanding results they achieved through trust, relentless hard work, and a passionate sense of mission and purpose, this team performed better than perhaps any in history. A small team with a leader who observes, knows the orientation of the situation, makes a decision, and then acts swiftly can save lives and also save companies.

ALIGNING BUSINESS CONSTRUCTS

Before we delve into the next COACH tool, let's go over a couple of organizational concepts. The first is *alignment*. To understand what this means, think about driving your car. If it's out of alignment and you take your hand off the steering wheel, the car will drift; you have to work hard to keep it centered in your lane. The same goes for a business organization. If it's out of alignment, it will drift in a direction you didn't intend. And just as misalignment causes wear and tear on car parts, it can cause wear and stress in parts of your organization.

The next concept is *constructs*, which are processes, procedures, structures, and policies. Examples include a policy on when to turn in timesheets, a software-testing protocol, and a reporting structure. When constructs support the broader goals of the organization, they keep an organization in alignment.

Over time, however, constructs can sometimes take on a life of their own and actually cause misalignment. One example is a business that enacts so many well-intentioned policies that it loses its entrepreneurial edge and drifts from the direction it wants to go.

Constructs can also help or hinder an organization's information flow. Information should flow freely up and down and around the organization, not just in one direction.

So before introducing a new construct to your project (or business unit or company), ask yourself a few questions:

- *Does the construct support and empower the organization?* For example, maybe a construct is being introduced because of compliance or governance issues. These are important issues, but you can't have so many associated constructs that your time to market explodes and you lose your competitive edge.

- *Does the construct help the organization serve customers?* Try to avoid constructs that serve only the internal needs of the organization. There is a natural tendency to increase the collection of managerial data over time. Verify that the effort to collect the data serves a customer need.

- *Will the construct build equity in the performance culture?* Sometimes, new constructs can interfere with the way high performance has traditionally been rewarded in your organization. Employees in a high-performance culture understand the need for business constructs but will support them only if they are aligned with their goals. When driving a high-performance vehicle, you learn to rely on both the feel of the car and the objective data. Your feel for how the vehicle handles a severe curve at high speeds needs to correspond with the engine sounds and the readings of your gauges. Constructs that would cause employees to slow down and document performance, although useful, will often be rejected by a high-performance culture.

CREATING THE NEXT GENERATION OF LEADERS

Current leaders can and should help create an environment that nurtures the development of the next generation of leadership. Such an environment blends a sense of stewardship and ownership.

Stewardship, at the most basic level, is about taking care of something that belongs to someone else. Historically, stewardship in business has meant the act of managing someone else's property, finances, or affairs. In an organizational setting today, stewardship implies that you focus not just on your own needs but also on the duties that you owe other people and the organization as a whole.

A culture of ownership is what it sounds like: even if you do not own the company, you value having ownership of projects, processes, customer relationships, and, yes, problems too. In this type of culture, you have to think and act like an owner. You have a line of sight: you can see a direct connection between what you do every day and the performance of the company as a whole.

In a culture of ownership, you will share information and information will be shared with you about the financial elements of the project, unit, or company. You'll know what it means to be late or early with deliverables or to have a happy or unhappy customer in terms of hard dollars and cents. You also will have a share in both the pocketbook and psychic incentives working in that organization; pocketbook incentives impact the wallet, while psychic incentives impact the heart. And you'll be involved in opportunities for meaningful conversations about how things will work in the future.

Building a culture that blends stewardship and ownership has real benefits. This model is already in place in many professional services and other project-based organizations. These businesses can generate high customer satisfaction and serve as great places to work.

HAVING A HIGHER PURPOSE

As an organizational leader—whether you're leading a team, project, business unit, or company—you have to understand your higher purpose. This purpose has to be something that transcends the routine of daily work and inspires all people to do their best.

General George Patton, of World War II fame, provides a great example of this COACH tool. His higher purpose was to someday lead a great army to victory, and he did eventually. Until then, his purpose sustained him. It got him out of bed in the morning through long years of drudgery at posts in remote parts of the world.

Good business examples of a higher purpose are plentiful. For example, Amazon wants to be the world's most customer-centric company. King Arthur Flour wants to spread the joy of baking to everyone. Zappos's higher purpose is to deliver happiness around the world.

The CEO of a technical training company told me an interesting story of how he discovered the best way to communicate his company's higher purpose. He was struggling to find the right balance of vision and reality because he didn't feel the firm's work would sound very inspiring. But the firm does training for hospital clients, so he used that as a starting point. He decided his company's higher purpose is to help clients create a safer, more efficient place to deliver healthcare. Saving lives is certainly much more inspiring than writing training plans!

At its most basic, a higher purpose is a reason for being. But it should also include a vision of the future. You want people to get excited about it, so it should definitely be bold. (Who wants to be the world's most compliant company or the one that best meets customer's needs?) You don't need to have a lot of data behind it; it just needs to be possible. Google's higher purpose is a good example: Google wants to organize the world's information. It's bold and it's possible.

You should constantly communicate about your vision of the future. But in articulating the story, remember to respect the past. If something didn't go well in the past, acknowledge the issue or mistake; don't hide it in the closet. Also, talk frankly about the present. For example, point out constraints such as regulations and timelines that will challenge the team in fulfilling the vision.

Finally, find a way to be passionate about the future. During one off-site training session, the participants were giving "stump speeches" about their higher purpose. (Stump speeches are short but powerful expressions of a company's past, present, and future. Like politicians, leaders should always be ready to deliver their stump speeches.) I still remember one project leader who spoke about his passion for his work. He did pretty much the same work as the other speakers, but people responded the most to his speech. What set him apart was the passion.

Here's another example. During a strategic planning session with leaders from a nuclear energy company, the topic turned to vision statements. Their vision was about lowering the kilowatt-hour rate. Would this get you excited? Me neither. I got up and flicked the lights off and on and said, "Your point should be 'We're here to provide a safe, reliable source of energy for our grandkids.'"

Whatever your vision of the future, paint a word picture that inspires people. Here's an old story that demonstrates this point.

A tourist was walking through a city and saw two men doing similar jobs. The tourist asked one man what he was doing. He said,

"I'm laying bricks. I've been laying one brick on top of another for days and weeks and will keep laying one brick on top of another for days and weeks to come." The tourist was a bit discouraged but went up to the second man and asked him what he was doing. "I'm building a cathedral," said the man. "It's going to be a grand cathedral."

Now, both men had been laying bricks for days and weeks and would continue to lay bricks for days and weeks to come. But one was a bricklayer. The other was a cathedral builder.

Chapter 3

Teaming Up

In the sports world, we've seen some great team performances recently: the San Francisco Giants winning three World Series rings in five years, the Alabama Crimson Tide winning four national football championships in seven years, the New Zealand All Blacks winning the last two rugby world cups, and countless others.

The business world has its share of great team performances as well, but they don't get the same fanfare. Consider the agile software development team that rolls out one winning product after another or a facility support team that keeps an automated building functioning at peak performance. I'm sure you can think of examples from your own work experience.

Teams that have effective leadership, that are well designed, and that draw strength from the environment in which they operate can accomplish great things. The task of leading teams builds on the foundational concepts of leadership and teamwork. The techniques and tools outlined in this chapter will help you move your own team up the performance curve—so they're ready to accomplish great things for *your* organization. This takes "teaming up" to a whole new level.

THE THIRTY-THOUSAND-FOOT VIEW ON LEADERSHIP: WHAT CEOS BELIEVE

In writing an earlier book, *The Power of an Internal Franchise*, I interviewed nearly fifty CEOs who led profitable companies. I asked these successful CEOs what they thought they needed to do to get the most out of themselves and their organizations. You can use their to-do list as guidance for your own leadership behavior:

- *Develop the next generation of leaders.* Organizations need to develop the leadership skills of midlevel managers so that these people can enhance profitability now and be prepared to take the reins of leadership someday.

- *Increase knowledge, skills, and abilities.* This goes for *everyone* in the organization. Depending on a person's particular role, it could mean becoming more technically adept in a specific technology or increasing one's skills in interviewing, conflict management, or customer service.

- *Align performance with rewards.* Successful CEOs believe that when the company does well, all of its people should do well. The creation of a performance culture with a reward system aligned to company goals is a constant theme for most successful leaders.

- *Communicate the correct message all the time.* Leo Fox is the former president of Tenacity Solutions. Tenacity was a software services company that was purchased by Computer Sciences Corporation in 2014. While Fox was at the helm, he would open every all-hands meeting, every strategic planning session, and every company gathering with a simple message of what Tenacity was (a software services company) and what it was not (an aerospace company). Fox pounded this message home on a regular basis for ten years, and everyone in the company understood it. So learn from his experience. Always ask yourself, What are the most important points for your clients, your staff, your team, your vendors, and your company to know? And also consider if you are always communicating those messages correctly.

- *Create an engaged and empowered workforce.* "Engaged" and "empowered" are small words, but they refer to huge and powerful concepts in the business world. Engagement happens when you find that sweet spot where an employee's interest aligns with an employer's business opportunity. Leaders have to make sure it happens as often as possible by matching employees' interests with the right opportunities. Empowerment happens when leaders find ways for employees to act on their own with the appropriate knowledge, skills, and abilities to make good business decisions.

You're probably thinking that accomplishing everything these CEOs have on their to-do list is a pretty tall order. But a lot of it boils down to a concept articulated by one of my favorite business authors, Matthew Kelly. In his book *The Dream Manager,* Kelly says that to do your best as a leader, you must become the best version of yourself—and that includes helping everyone in the organization do the same.[1]

Interestingly, most of the CEOs I spoke with were from companies that were not only profitable but also made the lists of great places to work. Could it be that if employees feel better about their jobs, they will *do* a better job—leading to productivity that generates profits for their company?

THE VIEW ON THE GROUND: WORK ENVIRONMENT AND PRODUCTIVITY

If leaders were to nurture a great place to work, what would that work environment look like from the employees' perspective?

First, employees need to feel that they have the opportunity and tools to do what they do best every day. That means leaders should consider if employees are in the right role and have the right resources to do their best work.

Employees also need to believe that their fellow employees are committed to quality and success. Do people have a sense that everyone is in the same boat and that everyone is rowing in the same direction?

In addition, employees need to feel that their opinions count. This means they are listened to, they are heard, and that their leaders take action in response. Here's how it works from an employee's perspective: The employee thinks, "I see a problem in the organization and I'm going to talk to my boss about this." After speaking with the boss, the employee thinks, "The boss actually heard me." Finally, the employee knows the boss heard because three months later that problem doesn't exist anymore.

Employees also need to have a sense of connection between their work and their company's mission.

Those are the key aspects of a great work environment. Now we need to ask, can employee attitudes—their perception that they are (or are not) in a great place to work—really have a direct impact on the productivity and profitability of an organization?

Absolutely yes! In the book *12: The Elements of Great Managing*, Rodd Wagner and James Harter report on extensive research that supports this conclusion. Wagner and Harter surveyed 120 organizations to learn the relationship between employee attitudes and company performance. They found that productivity was 12 percent higher in companies that successfully nurtured all the aspects of a great work environment.[2]

The picture of a great place to work painted in these pages is of a rather entrepreneurial environment. But one caution: insecure leaders can stifle an entrepreneurial spirit through restrictive policies and procedures and other business constructs. Insecure leaders neglect to talk to their team about the spirit, the environment, and the attitude that they're trying to engender. Don't be one of those leaders. Know that you can influence the environment for the better, and if you do, you're likely to enhance productivity.

THE VIEW ON ADMIRED LEADERS

Just as we can learn from what successful CEOs have to say, we can also study and learn from the attributes of successful leaders everywhere, not just in the business world.

In 1999, the Gallup organization decided to create a twentieth-century most-admired-leaders list based on polling it had been doing since 1948, in which Americans were asked which man or woman they admired the most. The resulting list was fascinating in its diversity. It included social-justice crusaders such as Mother Teresa and Martin Luther King Jr., who changed the shape of history; political leaders such as John F. Kennedy and Winston Churchill; people who never held elected office, such as Helen Keller and Eleanor Roosevelt; religious leaders such as Billy Graham and Pope John Paul II; the scientist Albert Einstein; and many others.[3]

It makes you wonder, What's the common ground among these diverse leaders? What makes them so successful at inspiring others?

Jim Kouzes and Barry Posner, probably two of the most impressive leadership writers we have today, have some research-based answers to those questions. In their book *The Leadership Challenge*, they list the characteristics of admired leaders based on a series of worldwide surveys. While the list is long and each of the characteristics received some votes, what's really striking is this: in thirty years' worth of surveys, only *four* characteristics have continually received more than 50 percent of the votes:[4]

- *Honest.* In almost any survey that Kouzes and Posner conducted, being honest was selected more than any other leadership characteristic. So it's pretty clear from their research that people are more likely to follow someone—whether in the battlefield or in the boardroom, in the front office or on the front lines—if they believe that person is worthy of their trust.

- *Forward-looking.* People expect their leaders to have a sense of direction and a concern for the future of a project and their whole organization—in other words, the ability to envision the future. Leaders themselves usually cite this as one of their own best traits.

- *Inspiring.* We all expect a leader to be a bit of a cheerleader. (Who really wants to follow a Dreary Dan?) Leaders need to communicate their vision in a way that encourages and inspires followers so that, whatever the circumstances— even, for example, if expected deliverables are overdue or looming project deadlines seem unreachable—the leaders can breathe new life into the effort and get people to keep following them.

- *Competent.* Most of us see this characteristic as critical to leadership. I'm not talking about technical competence here. This refers to the leader's track record of accomplishment: in the past, did the leader deliver what was promised? This type of competence will inspire the confidence of followers.

These are the most valued leadership characteristics, say Kouzes and Posner. Another expert on leadership, John Kotter, comes at the question from a different perspective that complements the work of Kouzes and Posner.

In *The Leadership Factor*, Kotter identifies traits that we have had since we were children that may have an impact on what kind of leader we are now and what kind of leader we're going to turn out to be. His view is that these traits are shaped by our education, the exposure that we have to different leaders, and our career experiences, whether they're trial-and-error experiences or learnings from formal training programs.

Here are the four leadership traits that Kotter identified:[5]

- *Drive/energy level.* Kotter says a leader needs this trait to deal with the difficulties of producing change over a long period of time. Drive keeps a leader focused on the finish line, while energy is the modality to reach that goal. I work with entrepreneurs in my role as an advisory board member at the University of Maryland, Baltimore County (UMBC), bwtech@UMBC Research & Technology Park, and one thing these entrepreneurs have more than everybody else is drive and energy. They can generally see the finish line and outwork anybody, plus they have a tenacity that helps them make things happen, no matter the challenges they face.

- *Intelligence/intellectual skill.* Kotter also says that a leader has to have the basic intelligence and intellectual skill to assess and navigate a complex environment. This is true, but over the course of my career, I've rarely run into someone who doesn't have the basic intelligence to be a decent leader. Usually, other traits make or break a person as a leader.

- *Mental/emotional health.* Many times, if you don't have an understanding of your environment—including your feelings, your clients' feelings, and your team's feelings—you won't be able to respond correctly. In addition to your ability to pick up on social clues, the reality of any leadership role is that it will be fraught with a variety of obstacles. Some will be small, like missing a product deadline, and others will seem catastrophic, such as losing your largest client. Dealing with obstacles requires mental and emotional resilience.

- *Integrity.* We can all identify truly high-integrity people. For example, Professor Muhammad Yunus of Grameen Bank and Mother Teresa are two people whose work has received widespread acclaim for having high integrity and improving the lives of millions of people. But for most leaders, integrity is measured by the alignment of their intent with their actions. Of course, most people approach their work with the intent of doing a good job, but generally, when people focus on the outcome of their work rather than the performance of their duties, the results are better. Focusing on the outcomes means working with integrity. We might say that these leaders are "customer focused," but what drives them is their integrity and not their interpretation of their job responsibilities.

It's important to look at yourself to see how you rate on each of the leadership traits that Kotter has identified, as well as consider them as you begin to groom your company's next generation of leaders.

PROVEN LEADERSHIP PRACTICES

Possessing and developing certain innate strengths helps you become an effective leader. But you also need to use specific leadership practices that have been proven over time to increase your ability to lead people. Through their research, Kouzes and Posner have identified five practices of effective leadership. As you review them, you'll see themes in common with the observations on leadership that I've shared already:[6]

- *Challenging the status quo.* How many times have you tried to roll out a change of some sort, only to hear "That will never work here" or "That's not how we do it around here"? As a leader, you have to be comfortable standing up to that attitude. Moreover, you should always be looking for opportunities to change things up, experiment, and take some risks. That's how your business will improve.

- *Inspiring a shared vision.* You already know how important this practice is. As I mentioned in chapter 1, you need to communicate your vision of the future to inspire action. On a practical level, the trick is to get others to support that vision. To buy into your vision, people may need to see what's in it for them. What's the emotional hook, for example, that gets a talented person to decide to join your firm? What client or partner needs must you address to engage those organizations and get their support?

- *Aligning your constituents.* You may have heard the term "trying to herd cats." Let me break it to you: that's part of your job as a leader. You need to get all stakeholders to understand what the mission and vision are and nurture a collaborative environment so they can collectively determine the best path forward. You must also strengthen others to act by delegating power to them and encouraging their initiative.

- *Modeling behavior.* Kouzes and Posner call this "modeling the way," and it's one of the most powerful leadership practices. It's about setting examples for your team for everything from workplace procedures, dress, and meeting times to e-mail responses, deliverables, and product releases—in other words, everything that you may deal with as a leader and manager. I attended a meeting recently where a very experienced leader showed up with a written agenda, written action items that had come out of the previous meetings, a written introduction for the new players on the team, and a specific list of outcomes that he wanted from this meeting. He was modeling the way. He had done this a hundred times before and would continue to do this, and it would eventually become part of the culture.

- *Encouraging the heart.* This is the fun part. It's all about recognizing contributions and celebrating accomplishments. When you warm a person's heart with a little praise, you're keeping the flame of motivation glowing. This practice may not come naturally to everyone, however. High achievers, for example, may have the point of view that achievements are simply part of normal operations and don't need to be remarked on. Don't be lulled into a false sense of security by a team of high achievers. Even the coldest of hearts will benefit from encouragement delivered at just the right time.

Let me share an experience from my own life that shows how you can begin to shift your thinking to incorporate best practices. I was at my daughter's weekend lacrosse game, having left her teenage brothers at home with a list of chores to do at the house while I was gone. The boys called me at the game to ask about a few of the chores, and after the call, a friend sitting next to me said, "Well, what incentive do you use to get your boys to do these things?" My response: "I feed them!" My feeling was that it's what they should be doing anyhow.

But I thought about this on my way home that night and decided I probably should have set the tone a little differently. Instead of just leaving the boys a list of demands for them to take care of on my schedule, I could have had a conversation with them along the lines of "You know, I'd like you to bring in the lawn furniture because the weather's going to turn in the next month; I'm going to be busy, and I know *you* could be a big help." I could've shared the vision—the big picture of why these tasks should be done—and encouraged their hearts a little more.

THE LEADER-MANAGER DUALITY

Now that I've laid out all these leadership practices, you may be wondering how they relate to management activities. Leading and managing are two different functions, but they are aligned. Leadership is about having followers—getting people to understand and believe in your vision and to work with you to achieve your goal. Managing is more about administering and making sure the day-to-day activities are progressing as they should.

For example,

- When you challenge the process as a leader, you then have to implement and monitor any change you've made to that process as a manager.
- While you can inspire a shared vision as a leader, you must institute plans and budgets as a manager. For example, you can be visionary and say, "We're going to be a $100 million firm," but you still need to plan and budget for that if you want it to happen.
- As a leader, you need to align your constituents, and as a manager, you have to direct and organize your resources. Aligning constituents means ensuring that people are on the right teams, teams are moving in the right division, divisions are focused on the right customers, and so on. Managers are then responsible for ensuring that company resources such as labor and equipment are organized and pointed in the correct direction.
- As a leader, you need to model the way for the people who are following you, but as a manager, you will find yourself solving problems and controlling projects to make sure everything is on schedule and in line.
- If you're encouraging the heart as a leader, you also have to find ways as a manager to report and give feedback on the progress of the organization. Good leaders will motivate the team to put in the extra time, but managers need to ensure that timesheets are still submitted every Friday.

This leadership-management duality is summarized in table 3.1.

Leader	Manager
Challenge the status quo	Implement and monitor processes
Inspire a shared vision	Plan and build budgets
Align constituents	Direct and organize resources
Model the way	Solve problems and control projects
Encourage the heart	Report progress and give feedback

Table 3.1 Leadership and management comparison

Almost everyone is naturally better at one side of this equation than the other. Earlier in my career, I wanted to focus on just the leadership activities because that's where my interests and strengths were. But I realized that to be successful, I was going to have to develop the discipline to complete the management activities or surround myself with team members inclined to complete them. A balance of leadership and management capabilities is rarely found at an individual level, but it is a requirement at the organizational level. For example, if an organization is tilted toward strong management skills, you'll likely find that it is overcontrolling. This often happens at large institutions and large bureaucracies, sometimes in government. They have so many controls that leadership doesn't get a chance to drive anything.

On the other hand, if organizations have weak management and a lot of leadership—and this is often the case with start-ups—then you'll find problems as well. You'll see action that happens in fits and starts, a lot of new projects initiated but not completed, very little governance, and very little financial control. The environment can be very exciting for a period of time, but companies can't go on this way for very long.

Of course, far too many organizations have the wrong kind of balance—both weak leaders and weak managers. And they're not good places to be.

Too few organizations, in fact, have both strong leadership and strong management capabilities. Yet that's what every organization should strive for right now and seek to engender in its next generation of leaders.

TEAM DYNAMICS

To lead teams effectively, you need to understand the dynamics of teams.

Teams present great opportunity because they hold within their ranks a number of ideas and a variety of skill sets. They also have a special production capability: they have the size, the scale, and the scope to tackle a large volume of work, and they benefit from a division of labor. So we use teams to conquer big projects and challenges within the organization.

Team success requires a strong performance culture. You want a team that is committed to accomplishing goals and meeting milestones. This is a team that other talented individuals will want to join. We all know of teams that don't get much done but have fun and go to happy hour together every Friday, but that's not what we're talking about here. With successful teams, fun follows form: a team that achieves success is an engaged and happy team.

Certainly our Western culture, with its bias toward individualism, can undermine the idea of teamwork and a team culture of performance, but it doesn't have to. The team should find a way to embrace individual talents. For example, if you have an orchestra, you want the most accomplished musicians. If you interview someone for a technology team, you won't say, "This person's brilliant in a particular technology, but we can't use her because she's not going to fit well on the team." You'll find a way to make her brilliance work for the team.

As a team begins to work together, discipline becomes critical to getting the best from every individual. We see this in sports teams all the time; the members are all talented athletes in their own right, but they have the discipline to work together to run plays well. The same goes for teams in the workplace. Discipline creates the environment for team performance—an environment in which everyone on the team accepts that a project must start and end on time, stay under budget, and satisfy the stakeholder base.

And even though we all know that teams are a necessity in the workplace, people sometimes have resistance to joining a team. Here are some forms this resistance can take:

- *Lack of commitment.* Our culture celebrates people who do great things on their own, but we don't often celebrate great teams. Part of the problem is that sometimes the word "team" itself implies imprecision compared to what can be achieved by an individual. Perhaps you've had the common experience of e-mailing a group of people all at once and asking for a response, only to find no one responds because everyone thought someone else would. A group doesn't always work very well, and newly formed teams, in particular, may lack the precision that comes with clarity on goals and direction. When you experience these kinds of situations, committing to the idea of a team as a productive entity can be hard to do.

- *Personal discomfort and risk.* If you are a superstar in your organization, you may feel that joining a team puts your professional reputation at stake; you may think you'll be dragged along—and down—by others. We may claim to be "all for one and one for all," but generally this procurement masks the real belief—which, again, is grounded in our culture—that individuals matter more. To address this type of resistance, you have to find a higher purpose—remember the

H in the COACH mnemonic from chapter 2?—to inspire team commitment.

- *Weak organizational performance ethic.* Is a strong performance ethic part of a company's culture? If not—in other words, if teams aren't required to perform or aren't rewarded for performance—then why would you actually want to join a team in that company?

WHAT MAKES A REAL TEAM?

Not every group of people gathering around a conference table once a week to share updates is a team. As noted in chapter 2, a real team comprises a small number of people with complementary skills who are committed to a common purpose, common performance goals, and a common approach for which they hold themselves mutually accountable. Let's take a closer look at each of the elements that—when they all come together—make a team:

- *Small number.* The numbers can vary, but generally from two to twenty-five people constitute a team. A group of more than twenty-five gets unwieldy; people have trouble interacting and difficulty agreeing on specifics. One note: Even with a smaller number of members, you still need to think about how you run meetings. Don't just tell people to show up. Tell them why they're coming, how they should prepare, and what they should bring with them. If people don't see the purpose for a meeting, it will just feel like a chore to them.

- *Complementary skills.* These are important because they are how the work gets done—or, in the worst-case scenario, how the work doesn't get done. A team will usually need three different types of skills:

  » *Technical or functional expertise.* Every project has technical requirements that need to be met. Leaders must be able to assess the knowledge, skills, and abilities required to meet those technical requirements.

» *Problem-solving and decision-making skills.* Many times, teams comprise people who are great technicians but struggle at solving the business problem at hand. And if no one can make a decision, whether it's at a task level or a project level, then nothing gets done.

» *Interpersonal skills.* You need people who are willing to offer help, willing to get help, and willing to understand and be empathetic. The lack of interpersonal skills is probably the cause of most failures in teamwork.

• *Common purpose.* I've already talked about the need for every organization to have a higher purpose that inspires a little passion. This is true even at the team level. If the group members are just there for the paycheck, you have to work around that, but if you can find a common purpose— a meaning—for the project, they'll be able to cohere as a team. Try to articulate where the team's project fits in the company, how it serves the client base, and what part it plays in the overall direction of the corporation. Then you'll have a common purpose that people can buy into. As a leader, you can leverage this to set the tone and drive the aspirations of team members.

• *Common performance goals.* We know that having performance goals is important, but we also need to tie those performance goals to the purpose of the project and the overall performance of the organization. Having that line of sight is motivating; people work harder. Goals lacking purpose are hollow and uninspiring.

• *Common approach.* You don't want to reinvent the wheel with every work process. As the leader, you need to establish a common way of working from the outset and make sure your team understands it and commits to it. To establish a common approach, ask yourself the following questions:

» *What are the specific jobs to be done?* Is there a common way of doing them? For example, you should make sure that everybody who's a tester does the testing a certain way, everybody who writes documentation does it a certain way, and so on.

» *How are schedules going to be kept?* Are they going to be kept using a master schedule or a specific tool?

» *How are decisions going to be made?* Are they going to be made collaboratively or dictatorially?

» *How are people selected for team membership?* Do you, as a team leader, have control of this, or are people placed on your team without your input? It's important to know whether you have the authority to move people off your team.

» *How will any modifications be made?* Modifications can include changes to the project scope, the schedule, the budget, the customer interaction, or the team membership itself.

So pay attention to instilling a common approach for your team. If you don't, if it's just a one-off every time or if somebody gets special attention, you begin to sow the seeds of discontent among your team members—and it becomes more and more difficult to manage and lead them.

Chapter 4

Own It

Imagine an organization where all the people understand that what is good for them is also good for the company, they all have a line of sight between what they do every day and the performance of the company, and people at every level of the organization take ownership—ownership of their projects, their customers, their practice, their division, or even their entire company. This is an organization with a strong culture of ownership. In this kind of culture, ordinary people can accomplish extraordinary things.

In this chapter, you'll learn about best practices and tools that can help you empower every employee to be a true steward of the business—to really *own it*.

ALIGNING PEOPLE AND PURPOSE THROUGH CULTURE

I've spent much of the last twenty-five years thinking and writing about leadership and culture. Leaders can influence culture, and culture, in turn, plays a huge role in how an employee performs. Employees are most productive when they have the opportunity and tools to do what they do best every day, believe that they and their fellow employees are working toward the same goal, and feel that their opinions count. What's more, employees need to see a connection—have a line of sight—between what they do every day and the ultimate mission of the company.

However, nurturing the kind of environment that will help your organization attract and retain the right people and tap their full potential can be hard to do. For example, I consult with professional services and product development companies as well as engineering, architecture, and construction companies that are operating in a very challenging business space. They compete for every client and customer against smaller boutique companies that can be flexible on price and larger firms that have deep benches and resources. And clients are more demanding than ever. As I like to say, "Everybody's been to Disney World"—people know what good service is. Everybody's picked up an iPad or a smartphone and knows about great user experiences. Clients now think, "I deserve to have great products and great service. What are you going to do for me?" With these pressures, a company can easily get caught up in short-term results rather than focusing on long-term strategy. For example, a firm may want to bring in new people to build depth in a service delivery or product development team but lack the cash flow to do that. And focusing on building a great work environment for those now on staff, and probably overworked, is difficult when the firm is dealing with so many market pressures. The firm isn't necessarily blind about what's needed, but in the demanding world where it operates, the constraints are legion.

This situation is not unusual, however. The demands of constant change have brought fundamental challenges to all businesses. For example, the competitive landscape is changing everywhere. We now know we have to be lean, mean, fighting machines. We can have no fluff in our organizations, which means we all have to wear a number of different hats.

In this environment, not every element of the business understands the overall corporate objectives; leadership may be going in a direction that the staff doesn't know about. Young leaders are often not equipped with the right tools, and many businesses are still trying to use old industrial-era tools and techniques to address today's knowledge-era challenges, where information and knowledge are currency.

A culture of ownership can play a critical role in helping organizations navigate today's knowledge-based world. But creating such a culture involves a learning curve.

Consider the example of one of my prior employers, Boeing. Ten years ago, Boeing acquired the company I was working for. My colleagues and I went from working for a $100 million shop to being part of a $50 billion operation overnight. Boeing was good enough to send me, one of its newly acquired employees, to what I called the "Boeing charm school," a two-week executive leadership program. What struck me about this program was that the company was just *introducing* leadership concepts such as coaching, mentoring, and grooming people. These were not radical new concepts in the technology world I'd come from.

But then I thought about the world Boeing grew up in. It had operated—successfully—as a command-and-control style, highly directive organization for many years. Now it was in a new age—in which a whole software development team can pick up and go down the road to work for somebody else who offers a better environment—and its leaders realized that what they were doing was no longer working. But still, they were struggling with where they stood on a new leadership approach. They didn't know if a different way would work any better for the company. Many companies and leaders are conflicted about this challenge.

Their struggle was essentially this: how do you reconcile the employer's need to get things done with employees' need for a good work environment? You find the answer when you realize that the work environment—culture—can be purposeful. It's not just a nice thing to have. It's a way to help you drive the business. When you understand that, you will find ways to manage the natural employer-employee conflicts in a way that serves both employer and employee interests.

So think about how you, as a leader, can focus the norms and behaviors of your company toward a more purposeful culture. Ask yourself the following questions:

- Do you invest in processes or people?
- What style of leadership works best for your company and your industry?
- What are the cultural attributes inside your company, and what leadership style will work best with them?
- How do some of the cultural changes in society at large— such as a new generation entering the work world—impact your workforce and, ultimately, your productivity?
- What do your employees expect, and does that match your and your corporate leadership's expectations?

Here's an interesting story that shows a not-uncommon gap between what employers and employees expect. Recently, the COO of a midsize company told me that he couldn't get all his project leaders to come to a meeting at five o'clock in the afternoon; one of them actually used this excuse: "I can't come because that's the night of my fantasy football draft." As a fifty-six-year-old man myself, my jaw dropped when I heard this because I would never share that with my boss. But that's the new normal in many cases, and people of my generation have to get used to it.

With that in mind, let's deal specifically with how to build a culture of ownership, which can be used to help bridge these expectation gaps and drive your organization toward its higher purpose.

THE LAW OF THE ENTREPRENEUR

I'd like you to begin thinking about something I call the "law of the entrepreneur." An entrepreneur is someone who starts, owns, and manages his or her own business. Not surprisingly, the law of the entrepreneur says, "What's good for the business is good for me, and what's good for me is good for the business."

But if you are an employee of an organization, you may still take on this mind-set. Let's call you an "*intra*preneur." And when all employees take on this mind-set—when everyone in the organization thinks and acts like an owner of a part of the business—you have a culture of ownership. We're not talking about handing out equity compensation. It's more the idea that employees have a line of sight between what they're doing every day and the performance of the company.

How do you nurture that in your own company or your own team? Think about the people you lead. Can they see the connection between what they do every day and the performance of the company? Can they draw a line, no matter how jagged or oddly shaped, between their actions and whether the company is successful?

If not, how can you, as a leader, build that culture of ownership?

THE FIVE BELIEFS OF AN OWNERSHIP CULTURE

You can encourage five beliefs in your workplace so that the law of the entrepreneur actually begins to take hold:

- *First, your people need to believe in you as a leader.* They need to believe that you have the character and competency to lead.

- *Second, they need to believe in the purpose of the organization.* Could the world move along nicely without your organization, or is it really important that you're here? People want to believe they are doing something significant. Maybe your organization is able to solve a big government problem that makes the world a safer place, or maybe it's meeting a telecommunications need that will bring services to a whole new constituency.

- *Third, employees have to believe in your operating model.* It's basically the focus of your business, and it covers a lot of territory: operating parameters, key management indicators, the way you deliver service, and everything else that defines how your company works. Do employees actually believe in that model, and does it not make sense to them? They're going to question it from time to time—maybe they're comparing it to the operating model at their old company—so it had better stand up to scrutiny.

- *Fourth, employees need to believe there's a reward for them.* You can look at rewards from two different angles. There's the psychic income, which lets you tell yourself, "I like being here, I'm rewarded emotionally for it, and I'm thanked for my effort." We generally get up every day because of the psychic income. But you can't forget about the reward of pocketbook income either. Total compensation has to be fair.

- *Fifth, people have to believe that they're empowered to make decisions.* If they don't believe this, they won't show any initiative. A lot has been written over the last several years on the nature of work, and one of the great pieces was by Daniel Pink. In his book *Drive*, he lays out the premise that work has to have some level of autonomy to it, has to have a purpose, and has to have some level of complexity.[1] So think about your projects. Are they meaningful? Are they complex? Are they autonomous? Are people doing that kind of work in an environment where they feel empowered? If all those factors are present, employees will deliver—over and over and over again. If those factors are *not* present—if employees feel no excitement about their work—they may zone out, and you're not likely to see any innovation. And without good ideas from all levels of the organization (because all the good ideas don't come out of the corner office), a company is not going to thrive.

To nurture these five beliefs and move the culture forward, you need to create an environment of trust. However, here's a striking statistic: in the 2012 Towers Watson Global Workforce Study, only 48 percent of global workers surveyed said that they trust the competence of the job being done by their organizational leaders.[2]

This seems to reflect a larger societal issue. The University of Chicago's Booth School of Business and Northwestern University's Kellogg School of Management have developed the Financial Trust Index, which shows that we don't trust our large institutions— large corporations, governments, banks, insurance companies— any more than we trust the people whom we work for. Americans seem to be fed up with the excessive compensation and lack of integrity of top corporate managers. The 2014 index's collective measure of trust held steady from the previous year at 24 percent.[3] So as far as trust goes, we have our work cut out for us.

Yet trust can happen. Let me share with you a story about a company that shows how to earn trust. This was a midsized company that got almost all its revenue through subcontracting. The CEO told me that one year, the leaders decided that they were going to chase some business on their own. They identified three projects they wanted to take away from their prime contractors. The plan was vetted; the entire leadership team was brought into the process, not just the CEO. They also briefed the entire 150-person workforce on the plan. But then they lost all three projects they'd gone after, and on top of that, their prime contractors fired them from other projects. So this company lost about half its business in a three-month period. It was absolutely brutal.

So what happened afterward? Within two years, the company was bigger and more profitable than before with a number of its own prime contracts. How did it weather the downturn and recover so well? Looking back, the CEO attributed the company's success to sound communication—being open and honest about the plan from the get-go. Even when matters went south for a while, the leaders did something very tough to do: they had a staff meeting to tell people that they'd lost their gamble and there would be some consequences. Some people did leave the company at that point; the CEO described them as "the rats that jumped off the ship." But most stayed, and the CEO believed they were the only ones the organization really needed—the people who shared a sense of being in it together and wanting to succeed together. They were invested psychically in that company—they "owned it."

But let's look deeper. Why did people feel that sense of ownership? It's because trust was through the roof at that company! The CEO and his leadership team trusted their people with the truth, even when the truth was hard to hear. And the people trusted them in return and remained committed as a team. This story may give you some ideas on how to create a more trusting environment in your own workplace.

BUILDING OWNERSHIP THROUGH TRUST

To help you remember the elements that go into making a whole and vibrant culture of ownership—with trust as the foundation—you can use this TRUST mnemonic:

- **T**each
- **R**eward
- **U**nconditionally support
- **S**hare information
- **T**rust others and be trustworthy

TEACH

If you're traveling in a car with your staff, think of your car as your mobile classroom. If you're sitting down to lunch with folks in the cafeteria, it's your culinary classroom. You get the idea. A component of leadership is teaching people how things work, and it's a continual process. Every successful organization not only has a successful operating model but also makes sure that everyone understands and uses that model.

A number of years ago, my company teamed up with another firm, an Oracle provider, to pitch for some business from one particular client. We were meeting with the client when the question of project costs came up. The Oracle provider's representative threw out a number of $282,000, and I immediately thought, "Wait! That is such a specific number, not a ballpark figure at all. Where on earth did that come from?" I paused the meeting and invited the representative to step outside the conference room with me. Since we'd never worked with him or his company before, I had to find out, right then and there, if he knew whether the work could be done for the amount he quoted. It turns out that he just winged it—and he was the only person in his company who did pricing. It's no wonder! His was not exactly a process that you could reliably replicate.

In contrast, everybody in *my* company had a spreadsheet that project leaders took into the field to help them capture data. If they had a pricing conversation with a client, they'd say, "I'll get back to you in twenty-four hours" so they could return to the office and run the numbers, and clients were fine with that. Our spreadsheet was a tool that helped us operate, and we made sure everyone who went into the field knew the drill.

Teach as many people as you can how your company operates. It helps create that line of sight.

Let me share another example. King Arthur Flour hires people with all sorts of different competencies, but they *all* have to learn how to bake. They all have to understand the baking experience because this experience is what King Arthur Flour promotes to its customers. So whether a King Arthur Flour employee sells flour or finances flour or distributes flour, that employee will *also* understand the customer experience.

And consider this story about Chesapeake Packaging, a company that made cardboard boxes. The CEO was an early adopter of what's sometimes called "open book" management. He made sure every employee knew how the company worked and made its money. He'd recently won a contract with McCormick Spice and had told its leaders about his company's management style and culture. It made the McCormick Spice management folks want to take a plant tour and meet the team. The way the story goes—and this is folklore at Chesapeake Packaging—Johnny from cardboard press number six was charged with taking the CEO of McCormick Spice on the plant tour.

Evidently, Johnny was quite an interesting-looking character, with lots of tattoos and long hair, who wore his hat backward and a T-shirt with the sleeves ripped off. But Johnny explained just how the company worked, explained where and how it minimizes waste, and described many of the initiatives around saving power and going green early on, how the company services the customer, and how the sales force was motivated. In short, Johnny knew exactly how the company worked! It's a great story because it shows that the operating model wasn't just in the CEO's brain. He had taught it to everyone in the company.

REWARD

Different people define success differently. It could mean making a lot of money, working with fun people, taking on a challenging assignment, finding career or personal growth, or achieving work-life balance. But no matter what their personal job goals are, people need to see the connection between the success of the business and their ability to achieve those goals. Any reward system should establish and maintain this connection by tying personal compensation and rewards to company performance.

But how, exactly? I would suggest that you *don't* start where most people do, which is looking immediately at what can be measured easily, such as billable hours, number of service calls, source lines of code, or products produced. Instead, start by deciding which behaviors you want to reward. You need to figure out which behaviors align with your purpose and mission and drive value in your organization. These are the key indicators of success in your business, and these are what you should measure.

But be sure to validate your approach. Check that the behaviors that you're trying to get people to demonstrate are appropriate and clear. In other words, are you rewarding the right kinds of behavior? Does everybody know what those behaviors are and how they lead to rewards?

Also, check to see that your reward system is consistent with the company as a whole. In many companies, you'll find a conflict between the reward systems and the principles and values of the company. For example, a company might value being collegial, sharing, and trustworthy yet reward people only for the amount of revenue they produce. Yes, revenue is crucial, but some aspect of the reward system should also reinforce the company's values.

UNCONDITIONALLY SUPPORT

When leaders support employees unconditionally, employees have the ability to make some mistakes. They can't, of course, make the same mistakes over and over. That would be unacceptable. But they do have to be allowed some mistakes so that they'll be willing to take more initiative.

In other words, they need to feel empowered. In *The 3 Keys to Empowerment*, Ken Blanchard, John Carlos, and Alan Randolph describe empowerment as "a cutting-edge 'technology' that provides both the strategic advantage companies are seeking and the opportunity people are seeking."[4]

Here's a story from my own experience that illustrates empowerment—mistakes and all. With a few partners, I used to run a small company many years ago; it had about $5 million in revenue at the time. We signed a $965,000 contract with an air force agency, which was obviously a big contract for a company of our size. My colleague had been the one empowered by the company to sign the contract. But we realized later that it was something called a "completion contract," which meant we'd get paid only when the job was completed. We couldn't afford that, and we knew we were going to have a payroll issue. We had to bring some people into a conference room and tell them we couldn't pay them that week; they would have to wait a bit. Talk about challenging their trust in the company! We did eventually get some help from the bank and some relief through contract modifications. But even so, a few people did miss a paycheck.

It was a close call for the business, but it also provided the greatest teaching moment ever. At our next all-hands meeting, we shared the story with everyone. Our message was that it was okay to try new things. You can make a mistake (but not repeat the same mistake) if the mistake came through exercising initiative. The story became folklore in our company.

Here's one caveat about empowerment. Some people may *say* they want to empower you, but then, with the first mistake you make, you find yourself in trouble with them. If you're a leader, you can't reprimand someone like this. You have to maintain your support for the person who made a mistake.

This support is one of the preconditions to empowerment. The tacit understanding is that employees must have the authority to act, they must have enough information and knowledge to act appropriately, *and* the organization must support them when they do act. Without all these conditions, empowerment is just an empty promise to employees.

When you are trying to encourage empowerment, employ what I call "vulnerable leadership." The easiest way to explain this is to paint a picture of the opposite approach: in this scenario, you—the leader—are perfect, so all others have to be perfect if they want to get ahead. If people do make mistakes, they're afraid to talk about them or admit to being less than perfect. Then they begin to hide their mistakes—and the situation gets uglier and uglier. This sad sort of dynamic inevitably leads to negative outcomes.

However, if you do something like we did at my old company—sharing the story about the $965,000 completion contract—it makes you a little vulnerable but it also opens you up a bit to other people. Then they are not so afraid to be vulnerable. This means they are not afraid to share their mistakes. And this is key because you want them to be able to share those mistakes *early*—before matters get out of hand.

SHARE INFORMATION

Here's my rule of thumb: if it's not the secret formula for Coke or Pepsi—that is, it's not proprietary to your company—and it's not personal information, you should strongly consider sharing that information. Your people need to be equipped with information to make sound decisions in the field.

PricewaterhouseCoopers did a study some years back that I think is still quite relevant. The study found that the differentiator between the top 20 percent and the bottom 20 percent of companies was that the top companies "trusted empowered individuals to turn strategic aims into reality."[5] Think about that. People have to *know* the company's strategy and direction if you want them to act accordingly.

TRUST OTHERS AND BE TRUSTWORTHY

Trust starts at the top. As a leader, you must always be making and keeping commitments to build trust in your organization. As a young man I played a lot of rugby and came to appreciate the trust that underlies good rugby play. When you watch a well-conditioned and coordinated rugby team, you'll see that they are able to make blind passes. Without even looking, a player will pass the ball to his teammate and the teammate will catch it because he'll know instinctively where he should be on the field. This is a capability that depends on trust and familiarity bred from years of playing together.

Think what this kind of trust could mean in the business world. Imagine an entire organization moving at the pace of change while acting as one: a manager being able to delegate a task without hesitation, an employee being able to focus on an activity with complete trust that his work will be rewarded, a manager not having to delegate a task because his team has already anticipated the need and met it, an employee getting a raise or bonus outside the "appropriate" time of the year because the manager thought it was the right thing to do.

ARE YOU OPERATING AT THE SPEED OF TRUST?

Assume you've followed all the guidance of the TRUST mnemonic to foster a culture of ownership. How do you know that culture is beginning to stick—to take root in your project or in your organization?

Four sure signs are high levels of initiative, accountability, and team spirit and a laser-like external focus on customers and external markets. I will explain each of these below.

INITIATIVE

Stephen Covey identified six levels of initiative in his book *Principle-Centered Leadership*: wait until told, ask, recommend, ask and report immediately, ask and report occasionally, and act on your own.[6] And I'd suggest another, ultimate level of initiative: act like an owner.

You can trace the growth of employees as they move through these levels. Basically, low initiative is characterized by sitting around and waiting to be told what to do. On the flip side, high initiative is characterized by acting on your own. Employees naturally move through this progression as their skills grow and as they're challenged to exercise higher levels of initiative. And a strong, empowered culture is going to motivate them to progress more quickly.

Here's one simple example of moving someone to the next level. I used to have an employee who was in my office all the time, telling me what he was up to. He'd say, "I did this today!" or "How was that, Boss?" Finally I told him, in a nice way, to just give me a weekly wrap-up. He quickly moved from reporting immediately to reporting occasionally.

In *Leadership Is an Art*, Max DePree talks about initiative in an interesting way. He discusses a concept he calls "roving leadership." Roving leaders don't walk past something that needs doing; they take action. In a real culture of ownership, everyone is—or is on the way to being—a roving leader. DePree says that to build roving leaders on your team, create a supportive environment for them, encourage them, praise them publicly for their actions, and encourage roving leadership at every level of your team and at every level of your organization.[7]

ACCOUNTABILITY

If initiative is about taking action and setting things in motion, accountability is the willingness to take the credit or the blame for one's acts. Like initiative, a high level of accountability is essential for a strong culture of ownership.

Try plotting your organization's position on figure 4.1. This will give you a good idea of where your organization stands overall in its development of a culture of ownership.

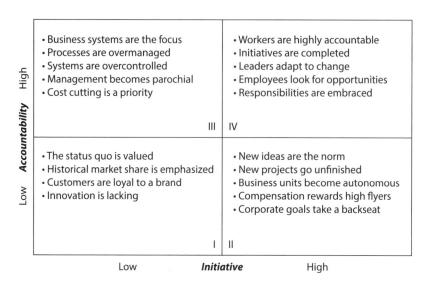

Figure 4.1 Organizational culture

If you ended up in quadrant I, with low initiative and low accountability, your organization values the status quo. It's probably a place where historical market share is emphasized; in other words, you've successfully served your customers before, so you don't feel that you have to change much. It is true that customers are generally loyal to a brand, but they can and do switch loyalties at any time, so they could leave your organization behind and leave you wondering what went wrong. Typically, this type of organization lacks the ability to innovate, and it's not generally a fun place to work.

If you found yourself in quadrant II, which is a high-initiative, low-accountability environment, it can be fun for a while. New ideas are the norm. Projects get started, but unfortunately, they often go unfinished. Each business unit tends to become autonomous, so not a lot of corporate sharing goes on—not a lot of cross-selling and up-selling, for example. The compensation rewards high flyers, so the real go-getters do well in this environment. However, corporate goals begin to take a backseat because the individual is emphasized. Eventually, things can begin to unravel because company governance and oversight never materialize.

If you found yourself in quadrant III, that means you have a low-initiative, high-accountability environment, where systems and processes become the focus. Management is important for the sake of management. A lot of reports are written, but you often wonder why they're needed. And instead of driving the top line, cost cutting becomes the priority. Not much innovation goes on inside the organization, and governance is over the top, so you may feel a bit stifled.

If you're fortunate enough to rate your organization as one with high initiative and high accountability (quadrant IV), what does that mean? Generally, workers are highly accountable, so initiatives are not just started but also *completed*. Leaders get comfortable with adapting to change, and everybody—leaders *and* their employees—is looking for opportunities and embracing responsibility. This is the kind of environment where you'll find a strong culture of ownership, and it's very exciting and rewarding.

Clearly, accountability is key to building a culture of ownership. So let me spend a little time talking about ways to create and increase accountability inside your own organization (or team or business unit). Here are a just a few tried-and-true best practices:

- When people are promoted into a leadership role, you can hand them cards that say, "The buck stops with you." It's a fun way to encourage people to be accountable for their business area.

- One company renamed its divisions "accountability centers," which meant that each center's leader was going to be accountable for that center's results.

- Another company set up a stand-up conference room. The implication was that when you go in there, you're going to get your work done—you're going to own it—and you're going to do it quickly.

- Another best practice is to create responsibilities, authorities, and accountabilities (RAAs) for each role. This way, people know what they're accountable for, what their responsibilities are, and over what areas they have authority.

One caveat: a lot of companies overuse the word "accountability." When you use it, be sure to define it so people know what it means—and know that you mean what you say.

TEAM SPIRIT

High team spirit is another signal of a strong culture of ownership. You can use the Help Model—anticipate the need, ask for help, become a servant leader, and show appreciation—as a force multiplier to raise team spirit and serve your customers at the highest level. Here's a closer look at each step of the model:

- *Anticipate the need.* Make every attempt to understand the situation you're in. The idea is to identify an issue *before* it turns into a blistering, bubbling cauldron of a problem so you'll be able to ask for help and allow time for a response from those willing to help you.

- *Ask for help.* Seeking out help doesn't make you less of a technician or a manager; it makes you *better.* Look at it this way: you can select an option and hope it will work out *or* you can call your counterpart in another business unit who's dealt with a similar problem and get help. The choice seems clear, but not all organizations embrace this approach. My strong belief is that, as a leader in today's rapidly changing world, you have to create an environment where it's okay to ask for help. Your employees don't have all the answers. The most experienced managers don't have all the answers. *No one* has all the answers.

When you're asking for help, make it as easy as possible for someone to respond. Be clear and concise, state exactly what you want, and explain how the outcome will affect the project or corporate goals. Also, if the request requires a significant time commitment, be prepared to build a short business case to support your request.

- *Become a servant leader.* This simply means that you begin to enjoy serving others—employees and customers, the community, and maybe even other people inside your industry—and you become sensitive to their needs. Servant leaders are great listeners, they have empathy, and they try to improve the other person's situation. Sometimes this means responding immediately to a request; at other times it might mean pointing someone in the right direction. It might also mean using persuasion; this can be your most effective tool. While serving others, you should also try to help them gain insight into their problems so they can begin to take ownership of them.

- *Show appreciation.* Acknowledging the help you've received and growing from that experience are important. When you show appreciation to someone who's helped you, make it public. A brief e-mail that copies the person's boss or a tweet thanking that person goes a long way in perpetuating the Help Model. A handshake in private sends a strong message, but a handshake in the presence of the helping person's supervisor supports and encourages the idea that serving others is a priority for the team.

  As you show appreciation, realize that the reason you needed help was that you are weak in some area of expertise. Resolve to mitigate that weakness by making it part of your personal development plan.

When the Help Model is used correctly, it has a profound impact on an organization. It's a way, especially in a world of constant change, to create synergies between individuals inside the business that will help it grow and adapt. It's really a win-win-win arrangement:

- *The company wins* because expertise is leveraged and gaps in service and product offerings are closed. Companies that leverage the Help Model go to market armed with courage and competency because they aggregate the intellectual capital of their entire workforce.

- *The employees win* because they have the opportunity to expand their personal competencies. They can attack the most difficult problems, call the most difficult client, and stretch their comfort zones with the full faith that their organization stands ready to assist them if a situation begins to go wrong.

- *The customers win* because the whole of the organization serving them is indeed greater than the sum of its parts.

EXTERNAL FOCUS

The last element that you need to achieve a truly effective culture of ownership is an external focus. Even if you've used the Help Model to create a great team spirit and you are operating in an environment of high accountability and high initiative, you won't have a truly effective culture if it's not also focused on the customers' needs.

Your mission is always about your customers; you never read a mission statement that says, "We're going to have the best inventory control process by the year 2020." Companies with an external focus will always expand their service to current customers as well as target new ventures and look for new markets, while companies with an internal focus build facilities to support the hierarchy within the company. Externally focused companies concentrate on increasing revenues, while internally focused companies concentrate on cutting costs.

The bottom line is this: the more externally focused an organization is, the more in tune it is with customers and the market. This is where business success happens.

Chapter 5

You're Branded

Think of a great leader you've admired—in any walk of life—and I'll show you someone who's surrounded by other great people who know how to get the job done.

Take John Wooden and Pat Summitt, both tremendously successful college basketball coaches. At UCLA, Wooden won eleven national titles, but it required the right talent, including 37 first-team All-Americans, 118 first-team All-Conference players, and 82 players who went on to the NBA. On the women's side, we have Summitt, whose University of Tennessee team won eight national titles, thanks in part to 21 first-team All-Americans and 39 players who later played professionally. Granted, Wooden and Summitt were great coaches and great leaders, but to rack up victories on the court, they also needed a talented team.

As a leader in the business world, you must attract and retain great people too. And believe me, the process can sometimes be as competitive as top-tier college basketball. To succeed, you need to understand what makes your workplace different from—and better than—other businesses in your labor market and sell your brand.

In this chapter, you'll learn how to build a credible and engaging workplace brand and how to help your employees understand and embrace your brand and everything it represents, including your culture and operating model. You'll also learn how to attract new talent that is the right match for your brand and business.

It comes down to this: greatness attracts greatness. When you combine a great brand and business with great people, you're positioned to lead your company to new heights.

CALLING ALL INTRAPRENEURS

In corporate workshops, I often divide the participants into two groups and ask one group to answer this question: "What words would you use to describe your most valued colleagues or most trusted employees?" Then I ask the other group this question: "What words would you use to describe the typical entrepreneur?" Neither group knows what the other has been asked, and each group answers its question in isolation.

The two groups then compare their results, and it is uncanny how often the lists are nearly identical. According to the words that have appeared over and over on these lists through the years, our most valued colleagues and trusted employees—just like entrepreneurs—are competent in their fields, show initiative, accept responsibility for their actions, and focus on the customer. The only consistent outlier is "risk taking." Most respondents don't use those words to describe their most valued colleague.

So it would seem that we do want entrepreneurial types inside our organizations, working with us and for us. These are the intrapreneurs introduced in chapter 4.

But where do we find them? Are we simply lucky if they dominate our ranks, or can they be grown? Is entrepreneurialism another one of those nature-or-nurture dilemmas? Is it possible to attract and hire people full of an engaged, entrepreneurial spirit? Can you create an environment that encourages entrepreneurialism?

The rest of this chapter will focus on these questions—and provide some answers.

WHO DO YOU THINK YOU ARE?
BRANDING YOUR WORKPLACE

One way to make your organization an attractive place to work—whether to attract new people or keep your current staff engaged—is to brand your workplace. Make people want to work there because they want to be a part of something cool, something big, something important.

Let's start by looking at the benefits of branding in the context you're probably most familiar with: the marketing of a product.

A well-branded product enjoys customer loyalty. Haven't you gone shopping for a new big-ticket item—a television, for example—only to find you're already leaning toward a certain brand you like, even if it costs a little more?

A brand also offers a means of differentiating a product in competitive markets. It can give you an opportunity to grab the attention of the customer.

In addition, brand loyalty can influence pricing. How many of us would be willing to pay $500 for the name-brand phone instead of $300 for a phone whose brand we've never heard of? Probably many of us would.

What about professional services brands? If your company's services were a well-established brand, could you leverage that to charge a premium or gain additional business? An old line in the technology industry used to be "You can't get fired for hiring IBM"—the brand behemoth at that time—and I'm here to tell you that was often true.

When I worked for Oracle in the '90s, we had a lot of beta products that we were trying to refine so they could access data across various computer platforms. I remember visiting Bell Atlantic Mobile Systems, an early Verizon mobile carrier, where I was in presales mode. I was trying to sell Bell Atlantic on our capabilities because Oracle, frankly, wasn't exactly hitting home runs at that time. Then Bell Atlantic called in IBM, which promptly sent twelve representatives to the same site. Needless to say, I had trouble defending against the IBM brand. The truth was, the Bell Atlantic leadership was comfortable with the IBM brand, so the rest of the staff felt, rightly so, that they were safe in going with it.

Many business decisions are based on comfort with a well-established brand.

Here's another example. At one company I used to work for, we were planning a divestiture and had to pick an investment banker to handle the transaction. I made a long list of candidates to consider—including small boutique banks, several midrange banks, and Bank of America. Guess who the boss chose? Yes, Bank of America. And if I had done my homework, I would have realized that he would do so. He drove a Cadillac, he rode a Harley-Davidson—he was someone who was always going to be most comfortable with the brand he knew.

Establishing a strong brand obviously has a lot of value, and that goes for your workplace too. When you compete for talent with a strong workplace brand, you'll get all the same benefits that accrue to well-branded products and services.

One of my client companies understood this well. At its offices, the leaders had set up a room they called the "Kool-Aid conference room." Why? The walls in that room were covered with plaques and photos and all kinds of other reminders about how great the company was as an employer—replete with blurbs such as "100 Greatest Places to Work List—5 Years in a Row!" This room is where they interviewed all their job candidates. This is where they met all their visitors. They wanted everyone to drink the Kool-Aid, as the saying goes, and buy into the idea that this company was a great place to work and to work with.

Here's one very important point to understand about having a strong brand. Whatever your brand promises—whether you're supposed to be the most reliable or the smartest or the fastest or the cheapest—you have to *prove* that over and over and over. If you don't deliver each time, you're in trouble.

Think about a job candidate who visits the company with the Kool-Aid conference room. That candidate is probably excited about going to work there. But the day after she comes on board, she gets chewed out for some kind of minor mistake. This kind of behavior won't keep a new hire engaged and believing in the brand for long. You've got to continue to prove the workplace brand—to truly live it every day.

You also have to customize your workplace brand. Many great places to work have a number of attributes in common, so you have to highlight those particular attributes that make *your* workplace stand out from the crowd.

Consider this example. A few years ago, I spoke with a senior executive of a consumer packaging company who complained that he had a hard time attracting the very best technical talent for his company's information systems department, even though he had his pick of top sales professionals. The problem was that the top technical talent simply didn't view his company as a particularly attractive option because it wasn't a leading-edge technology company. So to shape your list of workplace attributes into a brand, you might start by thinking of what type of employees you want to attract and retain.

You should also nurture an environment that allows for a brand that's both independent and inclusive.

Brand independence means the workplace has an identity separate from the leaders of the organization and even separate from the specific products and services offered. You may have a very dynamic and well-known product, you may have a very dynamic and well-known leader in your organization, but your workplace brand needs to stand on its own. People need to understand that it's unique.

Inclusiveness means everybody shares ownership of the brand. All employees feel they've played a part in shaping the organization and culture. It's not just a concept that's been declared by the leader. The brand is only as strong as the people who are part of it, and those people need to understand it, own it, and communicate it to others.

I recently led a workshop at a company that was trying to articulate its workplace brand. To help the participants with the process, I asked them what the key attributes of their work environment were. They said they were vendor agnostic (that is, they could work with a lot of different vendors); very agile in the way they develop programs; very dedicated; proud that every project was going to be successful; confident that they could meet commitments to their customers; confident of support from their executives; versatile; committed to promotion from within, with diverse career paths for technologists; client focused; well credentialed for the work they were doing; and in possession of a proven, documented work process. It was quite the list!

Next, I walked them through their list, and we identified the items that were unique to their company. They chose these attributes: vendor-agnostic environment, executive support, promotion from within, versatility, diverse career paths, and a documented work process. They felt that these attributes had been proven—over and over—and once you joined the firm, you would experience these for yourself.

In summary, they had come up with a workplace brand that was credible in the eyes of employees and credible to the customer base; customized, since that particular mix of attributes applied just to their company; and inclusive, because everybody in the organization bought into each of those attributes.

That's how an organization can define its workplace brand. Going forward, you also need to know how to communicate your brand so that it becomes a marketing tool to attract and retain the very best staff that you can find.

COMMUNICATING WHO YOU ARE AND WHAT YOU DO

At just about any social event you attend, whether it's a summer picnic or a holiday party, a ball game or a kids' soccer game, someone will inevitably ask you, "What do you do for a living, and where do you work?" Then you realize that answering the what-you-do part of that question means being able to talk about your business itself—your operating model—as well as your brand. Your operating model underlies the brand and is a miniature representation of the internal systems that keep your business running, your employees connected, and your customers happy. Understanding it and knowing how to talk about it are important for you, as a leader.

Let's focus for a moment on the concept of a system, which will then help me refine the definition of an operating model. I have an engineering and systems background, and in my world, we use a framework that may help: we think in terms of systems being simple, complicated, or complex.

A simple system is like a recipe. If you want to bake an apple pie and get the same result you did last time, you follow the same recipe. That means you use the same kind of apple and the same amount of sugar, flour, and other ingredients and put the pie in the oven for the same length of time at the same level of heat. A simple system equals a simple, consistent product.

A complicated system is like the one used to launch the space shuttle. There's still a recipe to follow, but it's more complicated because we've added advanced technologies, more people with varied competencies, and more factors that can be somewhat unpredictable, such as the weather. We know putting a rocket into space and bringing it back is doable, but risk is involved and something bad can happen. The team that follows this recipe needs a high level of expertise in a variety of fields to minimize risks and maximize the chance for success.

Expertise is also important if you're working with a complex system, but even with tremendous expertise on hand, the outcome is uncertain. You can't ensure success with a complex system. Parenting is an example. Imagine a photo of two smiling siblings, Liam and Lily. Liam may be a straight-A student and on his way to Harvard, but it doesn't mean that Lily is going to do the same. Even though these two share the same gene pool and were raised in the same household, many variables—differing innate strengths and personalities, differing outside influences, and so on—can't be controlled. You can parent both children the same way and you may indeed get a similar outcome, but often you will not.

If you're running a business, you'd like your operating model to reflect a simple system, which is obviously the easiest one to manage. But operations in most industries tend to fall in the complicated or complex space. As you learn to effectively communicate your operating model, strive to keep things as simple as possible.

What does the operating model look like in your world? To answer that, you can think about it in terms of four aspects: business focus, financial model, operating parameters, and core processes. Here's a closer look at each:

- *Business focus.* This starts with what you do and whom you do it for—your product or service and your customers. It also defines the promise you make the customers every time they make a purchase—what value you offer. You want everybody in your organization to understand this.

- *Financial model.* This is how your business makes money. Everybody on your team, everybody in your division, everybody in your company needs to contribute to the profitability of the business somehow, and the financial model shows how. (In the case of not-for-profit groups, this model clarifies the role that finances play in daily operations.)

- *Operational parameters.* These define what your business vision means operationally. They help your employees align their contribution to the daily success of the business and give those employees an opportunity to live that company vision every day.

- *Core processes.* These are the foundation of your project, your division, your business. When they are well defined, everyone understands what should happen in the operation every day. They are the engine that drives your business success. Everybody on your team has to understand these processes and constantly strive to improve them if you want to deliver long-term value to your customers.

When all the people in your company, on your project, and on your team understand what they do, whom they do it for, and how they contribute to the business's profitability, and when they execute core processes like an expert, you have a real opportunity for business success.

And to circle back to communication, make sure you are prepared to talk about your operating model and your brand, and keep the message as simple as possible. The more complicated you make the story, the more difficult it will be to grasp and the less likely it is to stick.

INFLUENCING ATTITUDES AND BEHAVIORS

If you want people in your organization to not only understand but also embrace your brand and operating model, you have to find ways to engage them. This starts with influencing attitudes so that the right behaviors will follow.

Consider this story from Peter W. Schutz, the former Porsche AG CEO, which centers around an early decision he made as CEO. In his first few weeks with the company, during a time of low profitability and even lower morale, Schutz met with the team responsible for entering Porsche in the upcoming Sebring auto race and asked about Porsche's chances for winning. To his surprise, the team said they had no chance of winning; they were entering the race only for promotional purposes and to test some of their new technologies.

What was Schutz's reaction? He quickly proclaimed that Porsche was never going to enter a race again except for the sole purpose of winning; he demanded that the team determine how they were going to win the race; and most powerfully, he said, "I want you back here at ten o'clock tomorrow morning to explain just how you're going to do that."[8]

After the fact, Schutz was actually a bit nervous about the strong stand he'd taken, but his instincts had been right. Word of those meetings leaked out to the racing world, and Schutz received calls from world-class drivers from around the globe. They wanted to join the team now that Porsche was serious about winning. The Porsche engineering group became engaged as well, coming up with creative ways to piece together parts from various Porsche models to make a real splash in the Sebring race. This story is a perfect example of how to attract and engage high-initiative, team-oriented, goal-driven people. People saw the possibility of success and a way to participate in it and acted accordingly.

Here's another story, from the consulting firm Pariveda Solutions in Dallas, Texas, which shows that letting employees know what's possible can begin with clarifying what's expected of them. The company's CEO, Bruce Ballangee, explained to me that he has a real passion for this issue and created what he calls the "expectations framework," which applies to everybody in the company. It's not an evaluation or a commentary on what you've done but rather a road map for what you need to do to progress. Everyone at Pariveda checks his or her progress against these expectations every few months.

The first expectation is effectiveness: can you solve problems and work with people? Another component of the expectation framework is business knowledge, which, in Pariveda's case, is the business of information technology: is your knowledge increasing and are you sharing your knowledge? A third expectation is putting others first: are you coaching and mentoring and serving the community? The next component involves your relationships and sales: have you developed an account plan, and are you able to grow your business? And the final expectation centers around leadership: do you have the key leadership abilities and attributes that are going to serve the company's stakeholders as well as contribute to your own career development? This approach has been a winner for Pariveda.

Why does this approach work? You have to first understand that people are *predisposed* to behave in a certain way. Their predispositions—that is, their attitudes—are influenced by emotions and beliefs. So to begin to change behaviors, we first have to address attitudes. And to do that, we have to appeal to emotions and beliefs by talking to people about the possibility of change. This is what Schutz did at Porsche. This is what Ballangee did at Pariveda. They revealed the possibilities. Their employees saw those possibilities as believable. And the desired behaviors eventually followed.

How can you get employees in your own organization to view something as possible? Employees need to hear stories of previous success. They need anecdotal evidence such as plaques on the wall, letters of appreciation, YouTube testimonials, or something else that shows that success has happened before in this company. And like those for your brand, these claims of success need to be true. In addition, you must be able to point to specific real-life examples of success, such as Tania over in project X, Sharon down in unit three, and George over in the southern division.

And you must constantly communicate about what is possible—at all-hands meetings, sales meetings, orientation sessions, and any other kind of gathering and via other communications tools you use. Only then will you get an attitudinal change. Nobody changes attitudes until he or she begins to see the possibilities for a different way.

Many societal cultures intuitively know the power of storytelling. The same stories of how things work are handed down from generation to generation. Inside a company, you also need to share your stories. We sometimes forget that a company is a culture unto itself and we don't focus enough on storytelling.

A key point is this: people will remember the stories; they won't remember the statistics. If I were a recruiter, I wouldn't brag about lowering the job placement rate by three points, I'd talk about past successes by people who walked through our doors. I'd talk about how we develop people so they can achieve success. I'd point to the plaques on the wall. I'd say, "This is how we help people grow. This could be you someday."

Now let me share a story *about* storytelling. A company hosted a summer picnic for its employees and their families each year. Right before one picnic, the leadership crafted a series of questions so they could be posed to employees at the picnic—such as why they liked working for the company and what was important about the place. But the questioners didn't stop with the employees. They asked everybody at the picnic—all the friends and little children and spouses of employees. You'd hear, "Why does your dad work at this company?" or "Why does your mom think this is such a great place to work?" Then the company compiled a terrific video montage of exactly what it was like to work there. A three- to four-minute version was shown before interviews, new-employee orientations, all-hands meetings, quarterly business meetings, and recruiting events. It was a resounding hit. People could see the possibilities for working at that company because these possibilities had been voiced in the video.

So the next time you have an all-hands gathering, grab the camera, circulate, and ask a few questions about your workplace—its training, work opportunities, culture, and more. You'll likely find you can put together a powerful story on why your organization is a great place to work.

And if you're serious about telling your organization's story, one book that you may find helpful is *The Leader's Guide to Storytelling* by Stephen Denning. It explains how to avoid jargon-filled corporate-speak and convey stories about your workplace and culture in a vibrant way that people will relate to and remember. Denning likes to say that the right kind of story at the right time can make an organization "stunningly vulnerable" to a new idea.[1] I like the term "stunningly vulnerable" because what you're really trying to do is get people to be *open* to the possibilities, so when they hear your story, the light bulb's going to go on inside their heads and they'll see what you see.

THE ENGAGEMENT GAME

Ultimately, you want everyone in your organization to be engaged with your brand and your business. Engaged people are committed to, active in, in sync with, involved in, and connected to what's happening in the organization. Webster's dictionary says people are engaged if they are "involved in activity; occupied or busy; greatly interested; committed."[2]

Why is engagement so important? The Gallup organization has good data showing that employee engagement is a real opportunity for organizations. For example, Gallup's Employee Engagement Index says only 31.5 percent of US-based employees are engaged. And while managers and executives fare somewhat better at a 38 percent engagement level, those sometimes hard-to-reach millennials are only 28 percent engaged. So while 31.5 percent of your employees may be engaged, 51 percent are not engaged, and 17.5 percent are actively disengaged.[3]

Employees in this last category—the actively disengaged—are likely the passive-aggressive ones whom we've all encountered at one time or another. They can be tough to work with, and as a group, they can erode your bottom line by dampening the spirit of other employees. Consider the Gallup data again: in the average working population, the ratio of engaged to actively disengaged is nearly 2:1. In contrast, world-class organizations with an engagement level of 64 percent have built a sustainable model of engaged employees. These organizations have an engagement ratio (engaged to disengaged) of closer to 9:1; for every one disengaged employee, there are nine engaged employees. If you aim to move your organization toward that award-winning benchmark, you can greatly reduce the negative effect of actively disengaged employees.

But sometimes those who are in the "not engaged" category can be just as harmful to an organization. They remind me of a quote from G. K. Chesterton, a popular English writer of the 1920s: "A dead thing can go with the stream, but only a living thing can go against it."[4] Those employees that just float along may not cause immediate serious harm to an organization but over time will cause the culture and workplace to atrophy.

The point is that the 68.5 percent of employees in most organizations are not engaged (51 percent not engaged plus 17.5 percent actively disengaged) and aren't making a positive difference in your company. And while this 68.5 percent figure represents the average company surveyed by Gallup, and your own company may have a lower percentage, it does seem to reveal a huge opportunity to improve engagement among your people.

EMPLOYEE ENGAGEMENT UP CLOSE

Now let's go deeper into the issue of employee engagement.

Figure 5.1 shows a chart where the y axis is interest and the x axis is opportunity. You'll also see that the chart is divided into four quadrants. If you map an employee's interest level and the business opportunities available to that employee, you can see which quadrant the employee falls in.

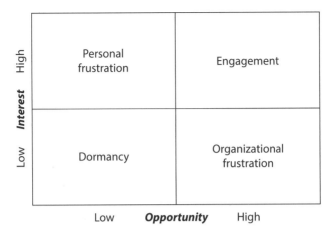

Figure 5.1 Employee engagement

The bottom left quadrant, labeled "dormancy," indicates a situation where opportunity does not exist and interest level is low. This may not mean that employees in this quadrant don't have interests, but it does mean that no one knows what those interests are. This kind of environment has very little opportunity for employee engagement.

The bottom right quadrant has high opportunity but low interest from employees; this is a recipe for organizational frustration. The organization has tons of opportunities, but your employees, frankly, just don't care about them.

On the other hand, perhaps employees have strong interests but are unable to find opportunities inside the organization that mesh with those interests. This means you're in the upper left quadrant, where employees feel personal frustration. Here, for example, an employer says to the employee, "I want you to get involved in proposals." And the employee replies, "I want to get involved in the industry group on Java script, so why are you telling me you want me involved in proposals? That's not what I want to do."

All organizations want, of course, to land firmly in the engagement quadrant in the upper right corner.

You can help make that happen. If you have direct reports, have conversations with each of them. Look at where the opportunities are inside your organization and see where your employees' interests lie. If alignment is lacking, you may have to create some opportunities to allay employee frustrations.

At this point, you may be wondering if engagement is really going to make your organization better. Are you going to be more efficient, more profitable? Are you going to be able to satisfy your customers better, and are you going to be able to attract and retain employees more effectively?

Consider what one high-profile business leader has to say about it. In a 2009 *Forbes* magazine article, Doug Conant, a former CEO of Campbell Soup, talked about the role of employee engagement in his ultimately successful effort to turn around Campbell's fortunes in the marketplace: "I saw that of all the measurable elements related to culture building, engagement correlates closest to shareholder returns. We can use engagement as a tool to measure our progress in building a high-performance culture and to set higher standards for our leaders."[5]

Here's a bit more background about the Campbell's story. Back in 2002, Gallup surveyed Campbell's employees and found that not only did 62 percent consider themselves not actively engaged in their jobs; but a full 12 percent felt like they were actively disengaged. Those numbers, according to Conant and Gallup, were the lowest ever for any Fortune 500 firm. But after twelve years of focusing on fixing employee engagement, the picture was far different: by 2014, 68 percent of all Campbell's employees said they were actively engaged, and just 3 percent said they were actively disengaged.[6] That's an engagement ratio of 23:1, which is absolutely incredible because Gallup considers a 12:1 ratio to be world class.

To be clear, Campbell's performance in the marketplace improved right in step with its increasing levels of employee engagement. So does engagement work? You bet it does!

Doug Conant also shares success stories about Campbell's in the terrific book he coauthored with Mette Norgaard titled *TouchPoints*. One technique that Campbell's managers use is particularly worth highlighting here. Conant says to bring a "How-can-I-help?" mentality to every interaction with employees and then do three things. First, listen intently to what's said and not said. Second, frame the conversation in a way that says, "Okay, I understand the issue; that's your issue, my issue, or our issue, and here's how we can advance it." Third, after you've had that conversation, say, "How did that go? Did I miss anything?" Conant found that with this technique, managers became more effective and these small moments with employees could have a big impact.[7]

What are you hearing from your people? Check out the following statements, which the Gallup research calls the "twelve elements of engaged employees":[8]

1. "I know what's expected of me at work." (You know employees are engaged if they know what's expected of them.)

2. "I have the materials and equipment I need to do my work right."

3. "At work, I have the opportunity to do what I do best every day." (This overlaps with findings from other research I've talked about.)

4. "In the last seven days, I've received recognition or praise for doing good work." (This, too, overlaps and confirms other research I've talked about.)

5. "My supervisor, or someone else at work, seems to care about me as a person."

6. "Someone at work encourages my development."

7. "At work, my opinions seem to count."

8. "The mission or purpose of my organization makes me feel my job is important."

9. "My associates or fellow employees are committed to doing quality work."

10. "I have a best friend at work."

11. "In the last six months, somebody at work has talked to me about my progress."

12. "This last year, I have had opportunities at work to learn and grow."

If your employees can make at least a few of these statements, you've got a chance to develop an engaged workforce.

THE HIRING PROCESS

It's one thing to assess engagement among your current employees. But how do you hire new people who will be the entrepreneurial employees you want—the people who will fit in and buy into your brand and vision?

Let's start by considering the case of Barb, a topnotch financial professional. I worked with her years ago when she was the chief financial officer for a midmarket software company. What are the upsides to hiring Barb? She's smart, she's organized, she's analytical, she's proactive, and she's results oriented. Barb also understands the mission of her company, and she has just about all the entrepreneurial attributes that you'd want in any chief financial officer.

However, when Barb decided to look for a new opportunity, she found herself in a difficult situation because she didn't have experience with one financial software package that was prevalent in her marketplace. (Her company had used another package.) Company after company passed on Barb because headhunters, recruiters, and human resources departments were unable to see past that gap in her résumé. Barb eventually landed a terrific job, but think about the many companies that opted for someone with the "perfect" résumé and therefore missed out on all the critical, cultural, and entrepreneurial attributes that Barb had to offer.

Most successful companies do realize that cultural fit is just as important as specific technical or professional skills. A project leader I used to work with called this the "get it" factor. The candidates he hired needed to have the technical competency to do their job, of course, but they also had to get the mission, get the purpose, get why they're on this planet, and get why the company is even in business.

An efficient way to identify the right candidate for *your* company is to think in terms of three goals. First, make sure the candidate is qualified; second, assess the candidate's cultural fit; and third, make sure you're educating the candidate. Let's look at each of these components in more detail.

QUALIFY THE CANDIDATE

Most of us are familiar with the first step. We invite candidates in and we interrogate them on their skills, their background, their credentials, and their expertise. But a lot of times this step gets overdone. Your job is to quickly identify the skills match. Of course, you should request transcripts and other documents to validate a candidate's credentials and do a background check or security clearance, but don't spend all your precious one-on-one interview time just rehashing the candidate's résumé.

Instead, spend more time on assessing aptitude. Make sure the candidate fits into how your company operates. Ask yourself, Does this candidate have an inherent understanding of the job we're trying to fill?

One extra bit of advice: don't fall in love with assessments. Mark Ehrnstein, the global vice president of human resources for Whole Foods, says his company discontinued using assessments during interviews because they were not as predictive as face-to-face interviews that documented personality traits and attitudes.[9]

And if you screen for specific leadership and management qualities, use behavioral-based questions. For example, encourage candidates to share anecdotes on how they've solved problems in the past. Or ask them to describe an example of leading a team to a specific goal. You might also ask candidates to describe an accomplishment and watch to see if the candidate is the star of the story or if the story is one of a team accomplishment that would suggest the candidate's good leadership.

ASSESS THE CANDIDATE'S CULTURE FIT

Once you know which candidates are technically capable of doing the work, think about whether they fit into your work environment and can embrace your operating model. Can they learn how you do business? Can they teach it to others? If you want to build a company that will grow beyond the personal reach and personalities of its current leaders, you need to hire and cultivate new evangelists. Ideally, these candidates should also be able to challenge and improve the business process. If candidates can do that from the outset, that's a bonus; if not, you'll need to teach the people you hire how to do it.

You can check for culture fit in the course of your interview. Ask the candidates if they understand how you do business. Have them tell you how their current projects work; their answers will indicate whether they'll grasp how projects work in your company. If they just follow procedures without really understanding the rationale, they may not be a good fit for your company.

EDUCATE THE CANDIDATE

Educating candidates occurs virtually every time you go through the interview process, even if you've decided that a candidate is not a match. Candidates have to understand your company and know what they're getting into. You want them to leave an interview thinking, "I really want to work for this company." The process should be similar to car lovers visiting a showroom to see the top-of-the-line Mercedes-Benz and thinking they'd really like to drive that car home. You want to be the must-have product, the go-to destination for potential employees—*the* great place to work in your industry.

The interview process provides an opportunity to sell your value proposition to prospective employees. Whether employment rates are high or low, all employment markets are seller markets. Smart companies don't consider themselves to be interviewing anymore; they screen, they assess, and they sell to make sure they get the very best talent in the door. Your value proposition is the essence of your brand. The interview is a great opportunity to present your brand and make it real to candidates.

Finally, once you've qualified, assessed, and educated the candidate, you want to try to close during this selling stage. Have a stump speech ready to deliver to every prospective employee. Describe your operating model, your business focus, your financial model, and the operating parameters of core processes, and talk about your business and how it's expanding and changing and how the candidate will have an opportunity to be a part of this changing and adapting culture of ownership. In other words, before you close, make sure that the candidate believes in your brand.

Before we leave this topic, here's a great technique for closing with a candidate you want to hire for your team. Imagine you're a candidate who's just gone through an interview process for a company you found very attractive. On your way home, you notice on your smartphone that you've received an e-mail from the company. You open it and, to your surprise, there's a video e-mail from the CEO of the company you just left! The CEO addresses you by name, references the staff you interviewed with, and lets you know the company plans to make a hiring decision right away.

How would you feel? Would you be a bit more inclined to accept an offer from that company? An e-mail like this is actually a relatively simple addition to any recruiting or interview process. Just prepare a short script for the CEO and shoot enough video—any simple recording device will do—for a ten-to-twenty-second clip.

Be sure to follow a few rules regarding the message. Make sure it's personal, and mention the candidate by name. Also be sure to make it relevant by talking about the position and the candidate's background. And send it out quickly, before the buzz of the interview wears off. You don't need to get carried away with production values because we're all pretty used to YouTube-quality video these days.

So try this video close with your next few candidates and see if you don't have a better chance of hiring the best in the marketplace for your team.

Remember, greatness attracts greatness.

Chapter 6

Trust Me

T rust: it may just be the most valuable asset you can possess in today's fast-moving and entrepreneurial business world. It is the foundation for a culture of ownership, which is crucial to an organization's success. You have to trust that the parts you need are going to be there on time, that your staff is going to show up prepared and ready to work, and that your boss is going to notice your extra effort and reward you in the future.

In this chapter, we will look at how trust is also the glue that holds together a successful client-advisor relationship. Becoming a trusted advisor to your client can lead to opportunities that your competition can only dream about.

Even if you are not currently in a product or services delivery role, this chapter will have relevance for you because the concepts will also apply to your relationships with your colleagues inside your organization. The term "client-advisor relationship" is used throughout this chapter and is meant to capture the essence of any customer interaction you or your team has.

WHAT DOES TRUST LOOK LIKE?

Trust can be a bit nebulous and hard to get your arms around. A great source on this topic is *The Trusted Advisor*, written by David Maister, Charles Green, and Robert Galford. Maister in particular spent his entire work life in the professional services world, managing and leading teams, and his experiences form the basis of this book. Over the years, many professional services firms of all shapes and sizes—including those in IT consulting, management consulting, and software development—have drawn on ideas from this book to help their staff build and improve relationships with their clients. I've used many of these concepts in my leadership workshops and as a source for this chapter.[1]

As you can tell from the title, *The Trusted Advisor* zeroes in on the concept of trust in a client-advisor relationship. So what does trust look like? I've asked my workshop participants that question for years, and they've been quite consistent in their answers.

Most said that they trusted people who were informed and experienced; seemed to have a stake in the outcome; were credible, knowledgeable, and even intimate with the work material; seemed to feel responsible and that their reputation was at stake; and had the data to support their comments. A good place for you to start on the path to becoming a trusted advisor is to simply ask yourself if you have these same attributes.

What if you *don't* have these attributes? Will people still believe you and follow you even if you don't seem trustworthy? Chances are, they won't. Trust is that crucial.

That's why the *Washington Post*'s Pinocchio scale has drawn a lot of attention in the political world. Named after the famous fictional character whose nose grew to gigantic proportions as his lies got bigger, the feature rates the latest political statements for truthfulness. The more Pinocchios a politician's statement gets, the less believable it is—and the less trusted that politician will be.

I'll admit that a few Pinocchios might not always slow down a politician. But in the business world—where we all have to get up and go to work and see the same people day after day—it's critical to be viewed as trustworthy if you want to have productive relationships.

So we're probably all agreed that we can't emulate Pinocchio if we want to inspire trust in others. But on a more serious note, who *does* seem trustworthy? When I've asked my workshop participants this question, parents and spouses—not surprisingly—are high on the list. Many also cite religious leaders and teachers. Civil servants such as firefighters are also considered trustworthy. And many do trust their work peers—or at least some of their peers. Supervisors often make the list too. So begin to think about who in *your* organization is someone to trust.

But what about the flip side? Whom do people tend *not* to trust? While a majority of Americans still have confidence in the police, a June 2015 Gallup poll indicated that our trust in that institution was at a twenty-two-year low.[2] Politicians—maybe no surprise here, given how they tend to fare on the Pinocchio scale—usually make it onto the least-trusted list. Others on the list include lawyers and salespeople and—not surprisingly—strangers. But acquaintances can show up on the list too if they tend to cry wolf, whine, or exaggerate.

Of course, this is a pretty rough cut. After all, I recently read that 85 percent of the public doesn't trust politicians, but that still means 15 percent of people do. I know some people who like their lawyers, and many salespeople have inspired great trust and loyalty in their customers too. You have to get beyond stereotypes and consider each person and his or her particular attributes individually to assess trustworthiness.

But how do you gain trust from others? Consider this very basic dictionary definition: trust is "the firm reliance on the integrity, ability, or character of a person."[3] Trust points to both character—with integrity as the central attribute—and competency, that is, ability. So to be trusted, you have to be reasonably competent at what you do *and* you have to have character if you want people to take your advice. The qualities of admired leaders discussed in chapter 3 are relevant to this conversation. Admired leaders are honest, forward-looking, inspiring, and competent. The same goes for an advisor. That's because becoming a trusted advisor is a form of leadership, and your client, along with your team or your staff, must be willing to follow you.

THE BENEFITS OF TRUST RELATIONSHIPS

What are some of the benefits of trust relationships? Generally speaking, when you hold a trusted advisor role with your client, you will be offered more business opportunities. As you build trust, you earn the chance to do more work for that client. Also, once you're a trusted advisor with one client, it's a bit easier to get references for new clients.

Even if you didn't hit a home run for your current client on the last project, you have a track record with that client and are likely to be given a second chance on a new project. You also tend to develop more influence with the client, and over time, deepening your competency in your chosen market segments supports your ability to shape the thoughts of the market-leading companies.

You can also accomplish goals faster. The more the client trusts you, the less the client feels the need to perform oversight and program management and the more the work can hum along without unnecessary hindrances.

Finally, a great benefit of being a trusted advisor is that your client will defend you against the competition. You will have additional insight on the next project and won't have to make the case for your involvement and your fee structure because your client will back you.

It's clear that all these benefits of trust relationships can add to your business's profitability. And the trust factor is important inside the workplace as well. In *The Speed of Trust*, Stephen M. R. Covey and Rebecca Merrill talk about the relationship of trust. They say that with trust, work gets done faster because everything doesn't have to be double-checked and triple-checked. Fewer conversations are held around what needs to be done. Less governance and oversight are needed because the feeling is "I trust you; you're going to get it done." And that all leads to more time for actual work.[4]

I saw a leader put this principle into action just the other day. I was in a business meeting when a division manager said to the company president, "I really need to get to San Antonio. Is it okay if I go?" The president replied, "How come you're not there now?" The company president's response let the manager and others in the organization know that they are trusted to make good decisions and they can act faster.

Before we move on, I want to share another insight from *The Speed of Trust*. The authors say that trust is, in fact, the seminal point of any relationship—the one factor that's common to well-functioning relationships, project teams, and companies. A loss of trust will certainly spell the downfall of a relationship, project, or company. But if trust is developed and leveraged, it can lead to great, even unparalleled, business success and, indeed, to success in all parts of our lives.[5]

THE EVOLUTION OF A TRUST RELATIONSHIP

Now let's zero in on how trust is built into the client-advisor relationship. Your client's trust in you is initially based on three factors:

- *Your reputation.* Think about a situation where you want to bring somebody new into a project and you ask your client to review the person's résumé. The client may tell you not to worry about it—if you know the person, that's good enough. This means you have a good reputation. You've done well for the client, so the client trusts that whomever you're bringing in is going to be the right person for the job. But with less trust, what might happen to that résumé? The review can be onerous and the project's speed may take a hit. Because of the delay, another contractor might have enough time to move in and get the work.

- *Your accomplishments.* Here's where you can leverage your track record, at least to a certain extent. If you've done some good work on a prior project, many times that can help you get the next project. It doesn't reflect a deep trust, but some amount of trust is working for you.

- *Your references.* Think about how great it is in a sales situation to be able to say, "Talk to Janis. We did the same type of work for her and it turned out great." Is this an arrow in your sales quiver? Be sure to use it—it helps the new client trust that you'll be right for the current project.

This is how trust starts. But how do you build on that trust and take your client relationship to the next level and then the next? Figure 6.1 illustrates how a client-advisor relationship can evolve. The x axis represents the depth of the personal relationship between you and the client, and the y axis charts the breadth of the business issues you handle with this client.

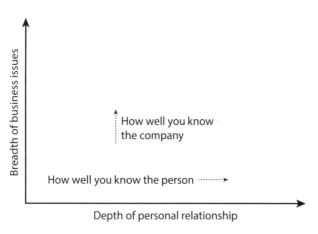

Figure 6.1 Client-advisor relationship

Let's focus on the personal relationship first. At the farthest left point on that axis, you're barely getting to know the client—you know the client's name, where the client's office is, and that's about it. On the far right side of that axis, you're pretty comfortable with the client and know a lot about her—maybe even intimate details such as the tuition for her child's private school, the fallout from her divorce, and more.

On the y axis, you can track the breadth of business issues that you deal with in this relationship. You're at the low end of the axis if you're involved in narrowly focused, specific activities for the client. You're high on the axis if you're dealing with issues related to the long-term strategy of the organization.

This basic framework will help you think about and assess where you are in a given client relationship. Be aware that you might bounce around on this chart, depending on which client you're focused on and even on the particular situation or project with that client. In other words, at some point, you're going to be in the upper right-hand part of the chart, in a deeply personal relationship *and* dealing with a strategic issue. But the very next day, you could be coming in to reconfigure a server for that same client—in other words, you've dropped back down the scale to work on a business issue that is less broad and does not require in-depth knowledge of the client. That's perfectly okay. You have to be comfortable with the fact that the relationship is fluid.

Now let's look more closely into the evolution of a client-advisor relationship. You can approach it from two different perspectives— the type of work you do and the type of relationship you have. But realize that these tend to go hand in hand. In other words, if you are operating at a strategic work level, you probably also have a strong and trusting personal relationship with that client.

First, let's look at how a relationship can evolve in terms of what business issues you are dealing with. This is shown on figure 6.2.

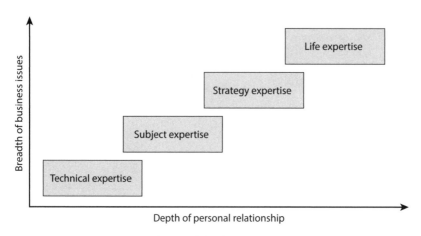

Figure 6.2 Evolution of the client-advisor relationship

You operate mostly in the lower left area of the chart if your client is relying on you primarily for your technical expertise. Take the example cited above, where you found yourself reconfiguring a server for the client. If this is the type of work you're doing consistently for a given client, you'd land here.

But you may evolve to become a subject expert (moving up and to the right on the chart). This means you are relied on for advice in at least one particular area, and you're also getting to know the client a little bit more. To stay with our server example, the conversations begin to change to the client's technology needs rather than this one server. Some sort of personal relationship is beginning to develop as well; you're having conversations that aren't only about a specific technology.

And then you keep evolving that relationship by beginning to talk about strategy issues. At this point, you're not just reconfiguring the server—you're having a discussion with the client about moving to the cloud rather than purchasing additional servers. Or you're discussing whether to outsource a piece of work or you're helping the client with a make-or-buy decision.

Finally, in a perfect client-advisor world, you achieve a strong relationship based on your life experiences (the far upper right area of the chart). What does this relationship look like? I think of it this way: At the end of the day, the client calls you on your way home and says, "I'm on my way to my son's ball game, but tomorrow my boss will want to know where I should spend that million dollars in the next fiscal year. Can you come in tomorrow morning so we can kick that around?"

To me, this is a great illustration of the trusted-advisor relationship. The client is comfortable enough with you to say, "I may not spend it all with you, but can you come in and help me understand how I can plan my budget?" You've expanded the boundaries of your original technical role and a trust relationship has developed. The client relies on all your life experiences and views you as an asset to her team.

That's one potential evolution of the client-advisor relationship, viewed through the prism of business issues. As I wrote earlier, you won't always be in a trusted-advisor mode; you have to be comfortable being at different levels of a relationship at different moments. But the idea is that—over time—you can build to a crescendo of trust that will help both you and your client capitalize on your relationship financially.

Next, let's trace the evolution of a relationship from the personal perspective by looking at types of relationships. This progression is shown on figure 6.3.

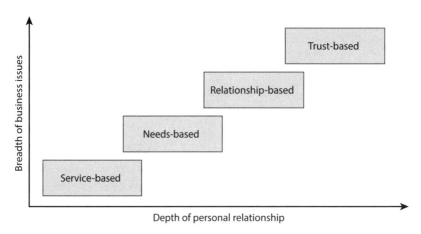

Figure 6.3 Client-advisor dynamic

Generally, you start with a service-based situation (lower left area of the chart), where your relationship with the client is mainly about completing certain specified tasks in your area of expertise.

Then the relationship can evolve to a needs-based one. At this point, the client begins to think in terms of what she needs, and you're beginning to think in terms of how you can anticipate and meet her needs. You're not just checking the boxes, so to speak. In this situation, for example, the project specifications may say you should deliver one thing to the client, but you've gotten to know more about what she wants as well as what she'll need now and in the future. You're getting some clarity about how better to serve her.

At the next level, you have a relationship-based situation. Based on past experiences working with you, the client now seeks you out and places her faith in you. She knows you have both the competency to perform the work and the character features that ensures the work will be done on time and on budget and will meet her expectations.

Finally, we reach the trust-based level. When we earlier traced the relationship from a business perspective, we called this the "life expertise" point on the chart.

What are the attributes of someone who has reached the point of being a trusted advisor? We'll cover that next.

CHARACTERISTICS OF TRUSTED ADVISORS

Think about these maxims:

- You do well by doing good.
- What goes around comes around.
- You reap what you sow.
- You can get everything you want in life by just helping enough people get what they want.

In one way or another, all these maxims get at what it means to be a trusted advisor: trusted advisors are able to focus on the client rather than themselves. This focus on the client requires enough self-confidence to listen, enough curiosity to inquire without supposing an answer, the willingness to see the client as an equal, and enough ego to be able to subordinate it to another's ego.

Let's drill down a bit to see how these characteristics play out, day in and day out. Here are some key behaviors and beliefs of trusted advisors:

- *Focus on the client as an individual, not a person fulfilling a role.* This doesn't always happen, of course. If you're starting work on a government project, for example, and you're already thinking, "When do we meet the contract officer on that project?" then you're thinking in terms of a role, not a person. You've already begun to say, "I'm not going to see Julius and Amy, whose dad just died of cancer and who is having a hard time making ends meet." You need to focus on the individual in the role.

- *Believe that a continued focus on problem definition and mastery is more important than technical or content mastery.* Be relentless in your search for problems and their root cause. For example, your team may respond to a service call to replace a motor on a chiller, but the problem may ultimately be electrical. Saving the client money by fixing a small electrical problem is a focus on the problem, not on showing your technical mastery of motor replacement.

- *Show a strong competitive drive aimed not at your competitors but at finding new ways to be of greater service to the client.* Basically, do you want to beat your competitors or are you there to serve the client and make the client's situation better? Sometimes you can do both. Sometimes it's in the client's best interest not to have a competitor offering its product or service to your customer. Other times, one of your competitors may have a solution that is just right for your client. The scenario is rarely cut and dried, but your client has to be confident that you have his best interest in mind— even if it may mean bringing in one of your competitors.

- *Consistently focus on doing the next right thing rather than on specific outcomes.* You can't pull the answer out of a playbook. Prefabricated solutions, although they may be a great method of selling your product or solution, represent a focus on your offering rather than the client's need.

- *Respond more to an internalized drive to do the right thing than to your organization's rewards or dynamics.* I've been in meetings, and you probably have too, where a consultant has said, "If I could close this deal now, it would really make my quarter." But consider how that is going to make the client feel.

- *View methodologies, models, techniques, and business processes as means to an end.* Use them if they work and discard them if they don't; the test is effectiveness for this client. And again, especially if you come with a quiver full of corporate-specific ways of engaging the client, this can be a challenge. But make the effort because your client can tell when you're using a one-size-fits-all approach rather than doing what's best for the client.

- *Believe that success in client relationships is tied to the accumulation of positive experiences.* Trusted advisors seek out—rather than avoid—client contacts and take personal risks with clients. This is *critical* and based on the flywheel effect described in chapter 1. You're not going to hit just one home run and right away become a trusted advisor. You have to have many wins that accumulate over time to build momentum and create credibility for you in the client's eyes.

- *Believe that selling and serving are part of professionalism.* In some organizations—often engineering businesses—"selling" is a dirty word. But if you believe in your offering, if you believe in what you do, and if you believe in your company, then selling and serving are integrated and have the same result: doing good for your client.

- *Believe that one's business life and private life are distinct but interconnected.* Trusted advisors recognize that they have refined skills in dealing with other people and that these skills are critical to both business and personal lives. They understand that the personal and the business worlds in fact overlap in many ways, and part of their job is to scope out the parameters for each client situation. Sometimes it's okay to talk with your client on weekends, and sometimes it's totally forbidden. Sometimes you can call a client in the evening or on the weekend, and sometimes you can't. Some methods of contact are okay during off hours, and some are not.

Trusted advisors transcend the boundaries of work-life balance. This balance is really a myth anyway, according to author Matthew

Kelly. In his book *Off Balance*, he asks us to dig deep and consider what really satisfies us and be prepared to ask ourselves some tough spiritual questions, such as these: "Are you overly concerned about what's in it for you?" "Do you confuse pleasure with happiness; do you even know the difference?" "Do you do the minimum amount of work to get by?" And Kelly doesn't address life in segments. It's not made up of work and family and sports and fitness and spiritual and financial and other categories. Instead, life is life, period.[6]

Kelly says that the more we learn to get beyond this balance myth, the better off we're going to be, the more satisfying our lives will be, and the more satisfying the relationships with our clients and our business world are going to be. My bottom line on the topic is this: the sooner you integrate the various components of your life, the better off you'll be.

THE TRUST EQUATION

At this point, let's step back and sum up the attributes of trust:

- Trust grows rather than simply appears.
- It builds over time, both positively and negatively; it doesn't just happen.
- It is both rational and emotional.
- It presumes a two-way relationship exists.
- It is intrinsically about a perceived risk.
- It is different for the client and the advisor.
- It is personal.

Of course, these attributes are variable and subjective. But if you are a quantitative type like me, you may be yearning for a way to measure the level of trust in a client-advisor relationship so that you can see where you stand and where you need to do some work.

This brings us to the "trust equation," which is illustrated in figure 6.4. This is a way to assess trust in a relationship by looking, in relative terms, at factors that have a positive impact on trust—such as credibility, reliability, and intimacy—in comparison to a factor that can have a negative impact, which is your level of self-orientation.

$$\text{Trust} = \frac{\text{Credibility} + \text{Reliability} + \text{Intimacy}}{\text{Self-orientation}}$$

Figure 6.4 The trust equation

Below is some detail on each of these factors. While you're reviewing it, think of yourself and your client situations so you can begin to get some insight into your own effectiveness as an advisor:

- *Credibility.* This is made up of your content expertise plus your presence. If you are credible, your client feels comfortable with you. Honesty and accuracy are key to establishing credibility. If you can get a testimonial from a client, it means you have credibility with that client.

- *Reliability.* Are you dependable, and can you be trusted to behave consistently? Reliability requires you to make and keep commitments, to make sure meetings have clear and specific goals, to understand the client's mission, and to always meet deadlines.

- *Intimacy.* Intimacy implies a willingness to talk about difficult agendas. The most common reason for failing to build trust is to leave out this intimacy—to be afraid to tread into sensitive areas about a personal issue, a schedule or budget problem, or a difficult relationship with a peer inside the client's organization. It's a delicate balance: you need to connect emotionally with the client, but you also have to watch that you're not pushing too far. You have to get close to—but not cross over—that line.

- *Self-orientation.* This factor comes down to whether you are more interested in yourself or in trying to be of service to

the client. Your self-orientation is considered to be high—
and will have a negative impact on trust—if you are constantly thinking about closing the deal, you have to be right
all the time, you are always looking ahead to the next great
opportunity or trying to sell new products and services, or
your financial incentives are known to the client. If you look
again at figure 6.4, you'll see that all the positives of credibility, reliability, and intimacy can be diluted not at all, a little,
or a lot, depending on your level of self-orientation. So the
more you have the client's interests at heart, the higher the
trust.

But I bet you're still wondering, "Can I really quantify all these
factors to make the trust equation work for me?" You can, using the
information in table 6.1.

Credibility	Reliability	Intimacy	Self-orientation
I am always honest.	I make real commitments.	I know the personal situation of the client.	I am constantly thinking about closing the deal.
I have never lied to the client.	I keep all my commitments.	I'm not afraid of becoming involved.	I enjoy being right.
My (our) work is accurate.	Meetings have clear goals.	I have an emotional connection to the client.	I am looking for the next great opportunity.
I am believable.	I meet milestones and deadlines.	I talk about difficult agendas.	I'm always trying to sell new products or services.
I can ask for a testimonial today.	I understand the client's goals.	I understand the client's work life situation.	The client is aware of my incentive plan.
Words, actions, and emotions			Motives

Table 6.1 Breaking down the trust equation

In the table, you'll see four columns labeled "Credibility," "Reliability," "Intimacy," and "Self-orientation." Under each column heading, put a checkmark next to each statement that applies to you and then count the marks in each column. If, for example, you check all five points under "Credibility," you'd have a score of five to plug into the trust equation.

When you assess each of the statements, especially those concerning self-orientation, make sure you do so from the client's perspective. In other words, what do you think the client would answer for each of these items?

When you have all the values to plug into the trust equation, do the calculation to get your score. The higher the score, the more trustworthy your client views you to be. (By the way, in case you score a zero in "Self-orientation," replace that score with a one to complete the division exercise.)

If you have a new client relationship, you'll likely have a fairly low score. Your credibility is probably not fully developed, and your reliability and intimacy are still on the low side because you don't yet know the client very well. At this point, a client is probably thinking you have your own interest in mind more than his, so that too will mean underdeveloped trust.

How about an existing client relationship? Trust tends to increase over time, so if it's a longstanding relationship, you might expect to have a higher score for credibility, reliability, and intimacy. And your client may also ascribe more positive motives to you, so your self-orientation won't be a big negative impact. This would be a strong trust relationship.

As you review your client-advisor relationships, think in terms of where you started, where you are now, and what you can do to continue to move toward that trusted-advisor role. It's well worth the effort because client-advisor relationships based on high trust tend to generate profits. You'll benefit from the success of your current project, and you will also likely get new business based on referrals or testimonials from your existing client.

INCREASING TRUST

You can build trust in a client-advisor relationship by using the following framework to work through your projects:

1. *Engage.* As you engage, your attention becomes focused and the client begins to understand that you have some knowledge that she wants from you. How did you get to this engagement point? It might be because of your résumé (knowledge, skills, and abilities), because somebody referred you, or because of your reputation. But somehow you earned the right to engage with the client and begin building trust.

2. *Listen.* In this stage, you acknowledge that the client has a challenge and the client affirms that you might have the potential to help. The client begins to think, "I'm being listened to, and this is good." Be aware that many times the client is already certain of the problem and is thinking in terms of different ways to solve it, whereas you want to listen closely and clarify the problem and restate it to the client before moving on to a solution.

3. *Frame.* At this point, you begin to frame, or define, the situation. What is the root cause of this situation? Is that clearly and openly understood? Is there transparency in your conversation? The client should be thinking, "This is exactly why we're here, and this is whom I should be talking with." And you should begin to coalesce and organize your thoughts and should be thinking, "I'm beginning to understand the problem set, and these may be the steps we need to take to begin to solve the problem."

4. *Envision.* Next, you envision some alternatives and you either state them or write them on a paper, a chalkboard, a whiteboard, an easel, or some other media for communicating the possibilities to your client. The client begins to see light at the end of the tunnel, and you begin to get comfortable with the direction you envision. At this point, you start to think in terms of budgets and forecasts and milestones.

5. *Commit.* Finally, you reach a commitment stage where the steps that you're going to take are agreed on by both sides. The client begins to buy into the approach that you've recommended, and you kick off the project.

Each of these stages is critical to the development of trust between you and the client. So think about each of your clients and projects, assess the stage you're in currently, and then begin to identify specific actions you're going to take to move forward.

As you do so, remember the factors that positively impact trust—your credibility, reliability, and intimacy—and decide how you can work on and demonstrate these by your words, actions, and emotions. This will help the client develop additional trust in you. And be clear about your motives; you want the client to view you as interested in her, not yourself.

At the end of the day, you want to know that you possess the most valuable of assets—your client's complete trust.

Chapter 7

Tell Me What You Need

Every leader deals with a complex web of stakeholders. This is especially true if you operate in the middle management ranks. You have to manage the relationships you have with bosses and shareholders; you have to manage the relationships you have with customers, clients, vendors, and business owners; and you have to manage the relationships you have with your employees.

In short, you have to manage up, you have to manage across, and you have to manage down! And the stakes are high: how well you do this will go a long way in determining your ultimate effectiveness as a leader.

This is clearly *not* about leading from the corner office. This is about actively learning about and responding to each stakeholder's needs so you can reach the right business outcomes.

SERVING OUR STAKEHOLDERS

A number of years ago, I was a senior leader at Rapid System Solutions, an IT services company. Rapid got its start by teaming up with AT&T on large projects. Back then, AT&T sold NCR hardware, including what can only be described as a real dog of a computer called the 3B2. And the 3B2 was the hardware of choice on a huge project that AT&T had just landed with the Internal Revenue Service, bringing Rapid along as a subcontractor.

Early in the IRS project, I attended a meeting with colleagues from our development team, the IRS, and, of course, AT&T. The discussion came around to performance, and the technical lead from our development team started criticizing the 3B2 because its performance wasn't what it should be. He went on for a while—at least it seemed like quite a while to me—with lots of colorful remarks about the 3B2.

Everything he said was truthful. But was it useful? No. The next two weeks were a bizarre experience for me and my team as we went on bended knee to the IRS and to AT&T to try to salvage our relationships with them and stay on the project. We did it, but it was a close brush with disaster: at that time, our work with AT&T accounted for about half our total revenues.

Clearly, our technical lead didn't understand the stakeholders. Part of this was the project leader's fault and part of this was my fault; we'd always been comfortable having the young man at meetings because of his technical expertise, and neither of us had thought to educate him in advance about the impropriety of talking down the 3B2.

In addition, some life and work experience is necessary to understand the concept of stakeholders and their potential impact on everything we do. In our personal lives, we only gradually perceive how this works. As little children, we're very dependent; just about everything is done for us and given to us. Then we enter adolescence, and we feel very independent and very sure that we know everything. Then, eventually, we come to a point in our lives when we realize that we are all interdependent: I rely on you for some things; you rely on me for some things.

Our interdependence in the workspace is a reality we have to embrace and manage. Robert Greenleaf, an early expert on business leadership, brought tremendous insights to this issue, thanks to his own extensive work and life experience. Greenleaf had a long and successful career at AT&T, including about twenty years as the head of training, and he began writing books on leadership only after he retired from the corporate world, setting the stage for later thinkers and writers on business leadership such as John Kotter, Jim Collins, and Warren Bennis.

Greenleaf's seminal work is *The Servant as Leader*. As you might guess from the title, he sees the role of a leader as one who serves. Here's one of my favorite quotes from Greenleaf:

> The servant leader is servant first. . . . It begins with the natural feeling that one wants to serve, to serve first. Then conscious choice brings one to aspire to lead. That person is sharply different from one who is leader first, perhaps because of the need to assuage an unusual power drive or to acquire material possessions. . . . The leader-first and the servant-first are two extreme types. Between them there are shadings and blends that are part of the infinite variety of human nature.[1]

Essentially, as a servant leader, you think in terms of giving people what they want as a means of leading and getting the outcome *you* want. You acknowledge that you can't always make unilateral demands. You accept that you have to accomplish goals through a variety of people, that these people all have an impact on you and your organization, and that you also have an impact on them.

The servant leader is a good model to keep in mind as you read the rest of this chapter on managing and leading stakeholders.

STAKEHOLDER LEADERSHIP

A stakeholder is a person, group, organization, or system that affects or can be affected by an organization's actions, including yours. Stakeholder leadership involves navigating a complex environment where you don't always have clear-cut authority and you have to know how to tap into your relationship-building skills if you want to make a difference and align your own goals with the goals and needs of stakeholders. As mentioned earlier, "interdependence" is the operative word.

This process is sometimes called "stakeholder management," but I see it as more nuanced and complicated than that. As I noted earlier, a manager oversees specific activities, but a leader guides people toward a common purpose. As a leader, you need to take an active role in the lives of people to nurture the outcomes of the programs and the projects you're working on and to create an impact.

Leading stakeholders involves four discrete steps:

1. Identifying your stakeholders
2. Understanding your stakeholders
3. Prioritizing stakeholder relationships
4. Developing and executing a plan to meet stakeholder needs

Each step is explained below.

IDENTIFYING YOUR STAKEHOLDERS

As a leader, you need to clearly identify the many stakeholders in your life. I've asked participants in my leadership workshops to generate a list of their stakeholders, in no particular order. Some of these might seem familiar to you: your boss, the government, senior executives, alliance partners, trade associations, coworkers, suppliers, the press, your team, lenders, interest groups, customers, analysts, the public, prospective customers, future recruits, the community, your family.

If you think this seems like too broad a list, consider this story. I was a young consultant at Booz Allen when I was asked to manage a proposal to a client for the first time. I got heavy support from a technical writer throughout the process: I sent frequent e-mails to him and called him, and he was very responsive. Then I learned he had been on vacation during much of the time he was writing. I sent his wife flowers and apologized to her, explaining that I wasn't aware I was infringing on their family time. After all, she'd been affected and she was certainly in a position to influence her spouse, so she too could be considered a stakeholder in my effort to produce a winning proposal. And my gesture did have an impact on her. That was twenty years ago, and to this day, whenever I see that woman, she says, "I remember that time you sent flowers."

UNDERSTANDING YOUR STAKEHOLDERS

Once you've scoped out who your stakeholders are, how do you go about understanding them better? Consider what financial or emotional interest they have in the outcome of your work—positive or negative. For example, does your team see a project as insignificant, or is it critical to their careers? For your clients—especially private-sector clients—how important is the financial impact? And how important is the mission impact for your clients, especially those in the public sector? Also consider what information your various stakeholders want or need and how they want to receive that information from you.

Next, ask yourself—though it may be uncomfortable to do so—what their current opinion of your work is. Is it good, bad, or indifferent? And who influences *their* opinions generally and their opinion of you in particular? That influencer is another stakeholder, so you have to understand him as well. If that influencer does not have a positive opinion about your work, you have to develop specific actions you can take to change his opinion. And if that person will not ever be positive—which might happen, for example, if you are an outside consultant and the influencer is loyal to a competitor of yours—how do you manage your way around that? What can you do to block that person so his influence doesn't get out of hand?

PRIORITIZING STAKEHOLDER RELATIONSHIPS

All stakeholders are not created equal, and there are only so many hours in the day, so you need to apply your understanding of each stakeholder to the process of prioritizing them in your work-load. How do you do that? Look at the stakeholder's influence and also consider the time frame in which you're operating.

Let's first have a deeper look at the factors that affect influence:

- *Power.* The first factor to consider is the stakeholder's power—whether it's positional power, power specified in a work contract, or power that flows from some other legal requirement that you do something for that stakeholder. Another aspect of power flows from emotional connection. For example, you may feel obligated to work with a particular stakeholder because you have a prior relationship or even familial ties.

- *Proximity.* The second way you can be influenced is through proximity. If you're doing work for somebody in another city or country, she may not loom so large in your daily ruminations and activities. But if you see someone every day, if you're walking by her office on a regular basis, then that means proximity is a factor and the stakeholder will likely have a lot of influence over you.

Time frame is another consideration in prioritizing your stakeholders. Here's an example. My son had to study for his finals. They were starting the next Tuesday, and he had the intervening Saturday, Sunday, and Monday to cram. He asked me to help him figure out how to prioritize his studies, so on Friday night, we went through this analysis: What's the first test on Tuesday? Physics and AP computer science, so start on those subjects tomorrow morning. What's on Wednesday? The French final. So review how to conjugate those French verbs *after* you've gone over physics and computer science. Then, on Wednesday, it's piano and orchestra—basically nothing to study for there. As you can see, the time frame helps you decide what to do first.

How do you balance and factor in both the time frame and the stakeholder's level of influence when you're trying to prioritize various stakeholders' needs? Figure 7.1 is a tool that can help you.

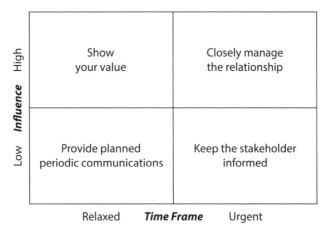

Figure 7.1 Prioritizing stakeholders

On this chart, the x axis tracks the time frame; a relaxed time frame is at the far left end and an urgent situation is on the far right. The y axis tracks stakeholder influence, with low influence at the bottom and high influence at the top. You can look at each of your stakeholders in terms of influence and the time frame of the work at hand, and then you can see which quadrant of the chart the stakeholder falls into.

Of course, a stakeholder's position on the chart can be somewhat fluid, depending on the point in time and what else is on your plate then. But the chart can guide you to a general approach for dealing with each stakeholder.

For example, if a stakeholder lands in the bottom left quadrant—relaxed time frame and low influence—consider providing planned periodic communications to that stakeholder. You may be able to get by with just a monthly review because the situation is not that intense.

If there are no urgent deliverables but the stakeholder is highly influential, you should look to the top left quadrant, where you'll see that it's key to show your value to that stakeholder. Why? Ask any service provider what happens to his value after the services have been rendered to his client. He'll tell you that his value drops precipitously in the eyes of that client once no deadline is looming. Even if you do good work for that client, as soon as you walk out the door, you're out of mind. No one is reminding that client of your value while you're gone. That's why successful service providers tend to adapt the professional presenters' approach to their own work. In presenting, the model is "Tell them what you're going to tell them, tell them, and then tell them what you told them." So as you provide your service, the mantra is "Tell them what you're going to do for them, do it for them, and then tell them what you did for them. And then tell them what you did for them, and then tell them what you did for them." You have to keep finding ways to show your value.

The challenge is different when you have a stakeholder in the bottom right quadrant: an urgent situation where the stakeholder has low influence. Here, you have to understand that this stakeholder still expects a lot from you and needs to keep informed. Whether you send a daily e-mail or make a weekly phone call, it has to be enough for the stakeholder, even if you feel stretched thin with multiple demands on your time.

Again, a consulting situation is a good illustration. Even though every client can't be your number-one priority, you don't want your prioritizing process to be too transparent. The worst thing your client can say to you is "I haven't seen you in a while. Oh, it must be the start of another quarter."

If you have a stakeholder who lands in the upper right quadrant—high influence and urgent timing—you must closely manage this relationship. Connect frequently, provide updates often, and watch like a hawk to ensure good progress on deliverables.

DEVELOPING AND EXECUTING A PLAN
TO MEET STAKEHOLDER NEEDS

Once you've identified your stakeholders, made sure that you understand what their needs and desires are, and scoped out a general approach for prioritizing and dealing with your stakeholders, it's time to develop a specific plan of action based on what they need or want from you and how you will satisfy that need or want. You'll probably find this easy to do for your number-one stakeholder. But the stakeholders that fall outside your top-five list present more of a challenge. These might be people you haven't spent much time with. But suppose you've encountered some problems on a project and a particular stakeholder's concerns have to be addressed. If you haven't thought much about this stakeholder, you may be in for a bumpy ride.

For example, imagine you are providing service to organization X and have a great relationship with Manuel in that organization but don't really know Manual's colleague, the technical director. Then you make a mistake six months into the project and that technical director is furious. Manuel says, "Aw, give the guy a break," but the technical director says, "Not on your life!" In this example, the technical director probably warranted a bit more of your time from the very beginning.

When you're trying to make specific plans to satisfy a stakeholder's needs, you need to consider three key issues:

- *Form.* What form of information does the stakeholder need to receive? Is it a report? Is it your swinging by and speaking to her? Also, is she expecting a blueprint or document or other physical deliverable?
- *Periodicity.* This is just a fancy way to say how often you have to meet with the stakeholder. How often does he have to see results from you? Do you need to submit a report at the end

of every day, every week, or every month? How often does he need to make contact with you?

- *Delivery method.* Consider how the stakeholder prefers to have information delivered. Some people like to hear information, and some need to read it. Some are good at interpreting spreadsheets, and some need to see a graphic presentation.

So make sure you understand the form, the periodicity, and the delivery method when you're communicating with stakeholders. Meeting their needs is much easier when you do.

The process of analyzing multiple stakeholders' information was introduced in figure 2.2. Now let's revisit that process and the accompanying planning tool, the stakeholder pie chart. Figure 7.2 is a blank chart that you can use to do your own planning.

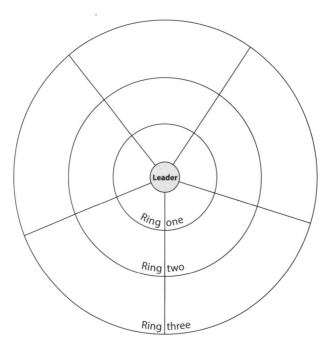

Figure 7.2 Stakeholder pie chart

Start by picturing yourself at the very center of the chart, in the leader's position. The first ring from the center, ring one, is where you list your stakeholders for a given project or initiative or organizational role. These are the people you've identified, made an effort to understand, and prioritized. Depending on your situation, you can fill in this ring with customers' names or the names of your direct reports, or you can show the categories of the various players (technical experts, client, vendors, etc.) on a specific project you have to manage. The more specific you are with stakeholders' names, the more impactful the plan will be.

In the next ring out, ring two, list each stakeholder's needs. Remember, you should have your servant-leader hat on and be very attuned to any specific needs.

In the outermost ring, ring three, list *exactly* what you're going to do to address each stakeholder's specific needs.

Let's look at figure 7.3, which shows a real-world example of how to use the stakeholder pie chart that came from a participant in one of my leadership workshops. In this example, Anna was the project leader. Her first ring of prioritized stakeholders included Janey, her boss; Frank, the client; Oscar, the vendor; Scott and Bob, the junior members of the project team; and Norma, the subcontractor. In ring two, Anna clearly identified what each of these stakeholders needed from her. Finally, in the outermost ring, Anna identified specific ways to deliver the benefits her stakeholders were expecting. For example, Anna felt that her client, Frank, would need a working installation completed by the end of the quarter, and as part of meeting that stakeholder need, she was going to call him each week after she sent him her formal weekly report.

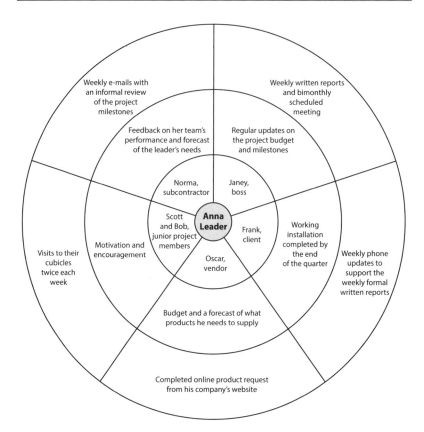

Figure 7.3 Sample stakeholder pie

Here's where you build on the general approach you scoped out in the process of prioritizing your stakeholders. You're now committing to specific forms—even specific communications content—a set periodicity, and defined delivery methods. It's here that you have to translate general goals into real-life nitty-gritty tactics—and follow through on them over time.

So, no excuses. You now have a process and a tool to help you anticipate and meet your stakeholders' needs—achieving the business results you want by being a true servant leader.

Chapter 8

Getting Your Message Across

Imagine you have a brilliant idea and your customer says that he's going to clear his calendar tomorrow so you can pitch it to him—and you'll have all the time you need. Or picture going to your boss's office, uninvited, to discuss a great client opportunity that just came up. The boss looks up at you and says, "Come on in. We'll spend a couple of hours brainstorming an approach."

It never happens, right? The world we live in is measured in 140-character tweets and thirty-second sound bites. Most likely, you're going to have a minute or two walking down a hallway with your customer, and you'll need to convince your boss via e-mail that you should pursue that great client opportunity.

How can you communicate effectively amid the frantic pace of today's business world? This chapter will tell you how to get your message across to any audience—and get the business results you need.

LOOK TO THE MASTERS

One of the most effective ways to hone your communication skills is to model them after someone from your past who's had a big impression on you. It might, for example, be a teacher, a parent, or even an industry or political leader who's an impactful communicator.

One of my favorites is Margaret Thatcher, the former British prime minister, a very forceful speaker with a strong delivery. It's no wonder that she was nicknamed the "Iron Lady." Then there's Thatcher's contemporary, former US president Ronald Reagan—known as the "Great Communicator" in his day. A former Hollywood actor, he was able to use his theatrical training to good effect in his speeches. He had a certain cadence and delivery that allowed him to charm people and put them in their comfort zone quickly. It's a good skill to have. If you listen to the political pundits today, they're often focused on whether a candidate can connect with the public.

In the business world, we have Bill Gates, a cofounder of Microsoft. He's very thoughtful—almost professorial—in his delivery. You can tell he's learned to think about the next sentence that he's going to utter because he knows he's one of those influential people who can move markets when they speak. You see the same deliberate style with Janet Yellen, US Federal Reserve chair, and Ben Bernanke, chair from 2006 to 2014.

In a totally different realm, we have Martin Luther King Jr., a truly inspirational speaker during the last century's civil rights era. Reach back even further in history to consider Winston Churchill, who's still famous for his nationwide motivational speeches to the British people during World War II. Churchill was not only influential in public speaking, he was also quite influential in small settings.

How were these accomplished speakers able to get traction with their audiences? How do marketers do it? How do writers do it? Read on and learn.

WHAT MAKES A "STICKY" POINT?

Many factors play into your success at getting your point to stick with your audience. First of all, the message needs to have a sense of urgency. Yell, "Fire!" and people will get that point fast and head for the nearest exit. Offer to develop a study on how to manage the eventuality of a fire and your message has much less stickiness.

Your point will also be more likely to stick if it conveys consequences. For example, if you tell people that bad things will happen if they don't do something, they'll be more likely to sit up, take notice, and take in your message.

If your point inspires fascination—if it's like a shiny object people can't take their eyes off of—it can also take hold more effectively. Similarly, it can stick if it generates excitement—that is, if it makes people feel they have to have that, do that, or be part of that.

A point or idea that's relevant now—that is important to the audience's life right now and may even require action—will also gain traction.

Sometimes you'll hear someone say, "It just resonates with me." Your idea could also stir an emotion of some sort. Even better is a personal connection: this occurs when someone hearing your idea doesn't feel as if you are talking to a roomful of people—she feels you are talking directly to her.

So when you're preparing for your next important communication—whether it's leading a team meeting or having a one-on-one with your boss—think about these different ways you can make your point stick. And remember this: you have very little time to engage people and keep them engaged, so you have to work fast.

YOU HAVE TO WORK FAST

I suggest a thirty-second rule, inspired by Milo O. Frank's book *How to Get Your Point Across in 30 Seconds or Less*. Thirty seconds is a somewhat arbitrary number, and it doesn't seem like very long at all, but it's actually a pretty realistic guideline. Busy businesspeople don't have a lot of time to spend listening to your messages. What's more, even if they'll give you the time of day, they'll lose interest quickly unless you are able to grab and keep their attention.

If you don't believe you really have to work that fast, consider how many times you have heard one of the following comments at work:

- "If he'd only gotten to the point."
- "All right, she's got five minutes."
- "I can't see him today. I don't have time."
- "She talked for an hour and I still don't know what she said."

When you think about your key point and how you can get it across quickly, you'll be a more effective communicator. My wife, Denise, loves to tell a story that illustrates this. As a division manager for Frito-Lay, she was meeting with an executive of Giant Food to persuade him to sell Lay's potato chips in his company's stores. She had her presentation—numerous PowerPoint slides—set up on her laptop in the conference room where they were meeting, and she also handed a hard copy to the executive so he could follow along. He picked up the hard copy, threw it in the trash, and said, "So, in a nutshell, why do I want to have Lay's in here?" Fortunately, she'd done so much preparation and was so excited about Frito-Lay products and Lay's potato chips that she was able to make her pitch quickly and effectively.

The situation she faced is not unusual in the business world. Challenges and roadblocks will be thrown up in front of you—from customers who are unwilling to listen and colleagues who don't have the time to focus on what you want to get across, to employees who are thinking, "I don't quite understand what you're asking me to do." So you have to know your content, you have to understand your argument, and you have to make sure that you are fully prepared *before* you engage.

A key challenge for all of us, in the business world and otherwise, is ever-present time constraints that we're conditioned to respond to. Our children take timed tests in school. The plumber is supposed to come at two o'clock on Thursday afternoon. And your big deliverable for a client is due next Monday. In other words, we all have to operate with looming milestones and deadlines at every turn.

Plus, our attention span is limited—and shrinking still more. Today's business cycle is shorter than ever. In the broader world, we tend to consume media in smaller and smaller bits of content. We expect television news to come in brief sound bites, and if we listen to the radio in the car, we switch from station to station. We even want our baseball games to be shorter. The digital revolution has only exacerbated this situation. We quickly move on from websites that we don't find interesting or engaging. We grab quick glances at our mobile screens during conversational pauses. We sometimes pay attention for only three or four seconds at a time.

When you consider all this, you can see how that thirty-second rule makes sense.

THE UPSIDE OF COMMUNICATING QUICKLY

One benefit of the pressure to communicate quickly is that it helps you focus your thinking, your writing, and your speaking.

I blog for a large telecommunications news site that wants me to keep posts to only 180 words. Staying within that limit focuses the mind. I can't say it's easy—in fact, getting the word count down that low can be brutal—but I always find that I deliver a to-the-point message.

Successful bloggers will tell you that you should always keep posts to no more than 300 words because if a post is longer than that, people will probably think, "I'll read it later" and click off the page. You can see this happening with workplace e-mails too. How many times have you gotten a message that lost your attention long before you even found out what the point was?

Being more aware of time constraints will begin to shape the way you approach and execute on communications—for the better. And you'll keep improving the more aware you are. For example, you'll tend to make sure that you keep your conversations on track, get in the habit of preparing your communications more rapidly, and often find that you've become more logical and concise in the way you structure your messages.

You're also going to shorten your interviews and meetings, giving you the wonderful gift of more time in your workday. You'll become a better listener as well. If you're prepared beforehand, then you're free to focus on the speaker's content—rather than anticipating answers in your mind—and can respond to what the person actually says. Overall, your increased focus and preparation will reinforce the strength of all your conversations and presentations.

In addition, once you make a habit of preparing well before you engage, you'll become more comfortable with the content, you'll more readily use open-ended questions to flush out conversational details to build your argument, and you'll also experience heightened confidence in your ability to navigate the churning waters of business communication.

And I promise you this: you'll get better results in your business life and even your personal life.

THE DOWNSIDE OF COMMUNICATING QUICKLY

John Wooden, the famous UCLA basketball coach, used to say, "Be quick—but don't hurry." In other words, if you're rushed, you tend to make mistakes or you don't accomplish as much as you'd hoped. It's the downside of speed.

When you're communicating quickly, this downside manifests itself a few different ways. For example, you can be viewed as impersonal. You might come off as cool and detached, and that turns off some people.

When you're in a hurry, you also might miss the nuances of some interpersonal communications. Did you notice if someone moved toward you or away from you as you spoke or crossed her legs or turned her face?

Finally, you may not have the ability to make the emotional connection that's usually required if you want to lead people to action. People change because they feel an emotional reason to change. People will do things for you because they have an emotional connection to you.

The challenge for you is to master the art of knowing when to use this quick-communication approach and when not to. Sometimes, for example, when you're starting a project with a new team, the personal connection may be the point. You have lunch together, you share some stories about family and children and where you worked before, and a bit of intimacy develops that's beneficial for all. But you don't always have the luxury of time that's required to do this.

More often, you won't have that luxury.

WHAT MAKES A SUCCESSFUL COMMUNICATION?

Why do some ideas stick while others don't? Below is a simple mnemonic, first presented in the book *Made to Stick* by Chip and Dan Heath, to help you remember key tools for making things stick:[1]

- **S**implicity
- **U**nexpectedness
- **C**oncreteness
- **C**redibility
- **E**motions
- **S**tories

You may be wondering if there should be another S in this SUCCES mnemonic. Nope. Without it, you still get the gist. The truncated acronym honors the idea that we're in a hurry and we're keeping it short, simple, and to the point.

SIMPLICITY

Simplicity is about finding the essential core of your idea. Anything that's too complex is going to blow you right past the thirty-second rule for getting your point across. And complex arguments are harder for your audience to follow and grab onto.

UNEXPECTEDNESS

Unexpectedness is about getting your audience to pay attention to your idea. This doesn't mean engaging in outlandish behavior, but it does mean using something that's a little different from the usual corporate approach. Can you create some kind of really engaging moment for the audience?

When I was running a company, my goal was to do something unexpected at every all-hands meeting. I tried a million ideas. Some worked and some didn't.

I started one meeting by saying, "Today we're not going to clap for anything. If you want to express approval today, blow a kazoo!" It was, indeed, unexpected, and I thought it would be a great way to get people involved. But I forgot another rule of communication: know your audience. These were 150 introverted engineers who thought that blowing a kazoo at a business meeting was the dumbest idea in the world, and they let me know it.

But sometimes I did find the right dash of unexpectedness. For example, shortly after my company was acquired by Boeing, I found myself leading a Boeing division with a revenue target of $103 million. This was in 2003, so I got a henna tattoo on my upper arm that said "103 in 03." Then I attended our Saturday team leadership meeting, where we usually discussed budgets. I had a workout shirt underneath my sweater, and when I pulled off the sweater, I got everyone's attention with that tattoo on my bicep. (Thankfully, I was in better shape back then.) Nobody left that room not knowing that $103 million was our revenue target for 2003, and none of them ever forgot it. So try to find a way to do something unexpected and achieve the impact you want.

CONCRETENESS

The fact that I had a specific concept to sell also helped me get my point across in that team meeting. You could call it a concreteness that makes an idea clear. It's tough to get across a vague point. This can be a particular challenge when you're explaining something like virtual solutions. Having a discussion about the cloud makes some folks' heads hurt because they can't wrap their brains around the concept. But you have to try—you have to make it real for people.

One of the key indicators in my previous software services company was the average billing rate we charged clients across all projects. During a leadership meeting, our chief financial officer shared that he just noticed we paid the clown we hired for the summer picnic a rate of $75 per hour. At that time, our average billing rate was $72 per hour. After we advertised that fact and our CFO presented those rates dressed in his best red nose and orange wig, our average billing rate soared. From then on, no project leader would ever price a project at rates below the "clown rate"!

CREDIBILITY

If you want people to believe your idea—to really buy into your message—you have to be credible. You establish credibility with your credentials—your position, degrees, training, and so on—as well as with your experiences and accomplishments. I was in a workshop recently, and the head of maintenance—someone whose work and reliability we all knew—came in and said, "A fire alarm is going off at nine o'clock. No reason to worry—we just want to practice our emergency procedures. I want you all to respond appropriately and leave the building." When the alarm went off, we felt pretty comfortable that it was indeed just a test and we followed the maintenance man's advice about leaving the building. This was because he was credible—he had the credentials, the experience, and the accomplishments that made us believe and then follow him.

EMOTIONS

Yet another element often plays into getting someone to accept your message: emotion. You have to get people to care about your idea. You've got to hit a nerve, strike a chord, get somebody excited or nervous or scared or frightened or hungry. So the next time you want to communicate an idea, think about what you might do to generate emotions in your audience.

This exercise may help you understand what I mean. First, imagine your doctor having a very scientifically based discussion with you about the causes of high cholesterol and ways to lower it. Then, imagine she says something like this instead: "Remember our neighbor John who died at fifty-two of a heart attack? I don't want you to be that guy. Here's what we can do to get your cholesterol down." If you heard that from your doctor, you would take whatever specific action she suggested to lower your cholesterol.

STORIES

The last element of the SUCCES mnemonic is stories. You should try to wrap up all the other elements of your message into a story. I like this definition from *How to Write Your Best Story*, by Philip Martin: "A story goes somewhere. It follows, with purpose, one or more characters through a series of events. By the end, it arrives at its target destination, fulfilling its reason for having been told." When you tell a story, it's easier for your audience to follow, remember, and repeat your idea to others—and get them to act on it.[2]

One of my favorite stories came from, of all places, the Department of Natural Resources in North Carolina. A number of years ago, North Carolina experienced shark attacks off its coast, so the department wanted to issue a communication that wouldn't discount the attacks but would put them in perspective because they were, in fact, quite rare. So they came up with a fabulous story, the gist of which is that more people in North Carolina are killed by Bambi than by Jaws. It was engaging, and its point stuck with me. And it stuck with a lot of other people because many folks still hit the beaches in North Carolina that summer (and there were no unpleasant sightings of Jaws or any of his relatives).

If you think about great communicators in general, they're good storytellers. They have a way of weaving their point into an anecdote that people can relate to and remember. Great orators throughout history—from Cicero to Lincoln—communicate via stories.

MESSAGES THAT HAVE STUCK

An effective message embodies the various elements highlighted in the SUCCES mnemonic. In this section, we'll look at some examples culled from politics, health, and business. Let's start with an example from politics. Back in the early 2000s, President George W. Bush delivered his famous "axis of evil" message. Combining the color of President Reagan's "evil empire" with a grim reminder of our World War II–era enemies, Bush's phrase really stuck. It was simple, unexpected, and concrete, and coming only months after the 9/11 terrorist attacks, it tapped into the country's greatest fears.

On the flip side of that is Bush's "mission to Mars" pitch. It may have been a noble idea—he seemed to want to echo JFK's call for us to put a man on the moon—but it lacked credibility. It was announced just before Bush's 2004 State of the Union address, with a war on and a struggling economy, so it just didn't seem feasible or believable.

On the health front, we have the success of the Atkins diet message, which caught on with many people. It was certainly unexpected: eat bacon cheeseburgers and lose weight! And everyone seemed to know someone who had success with it. On the other hand, the US Department of Agriculture's revised food pyramid didn't get people too stirred up about diet. It wasn't concrete and it wasn't simple. People weren't even clear on why it was called a "pyramid."

In terms of business messages, Johnson & Johnson's corporate credo works well. It says, "We believe our first responsibility is to the doctors, nurses, and patients, to mothers and fathers and all others who use our products and services."[3] Both concrete and emotional, it gives Johnson & Johnson workers an idea of what their priorities should be, no matter what role they hold in the company.

Contrast it with ExxonMobil's guiding principle: "ExxonMobil Corporation is committed to being the world's premier petroleum and petrochemical company. To that end, our goal is to continuously achieve superior financial and operating results while adhering to the highest standards of business conduct."[4] This message contains nothing exciting that's going to stick with an audience.

CRAFTING YOUR MESSAGE: THE BASICS

Now that you understand successful communications, you're ready to craft your own message. As you do, keep these three basic principles in mind:

- *Have a single clear-cut objective.* Know what you want to accomplish with this communication. What's your goal, your purpose, your destination? Think about what you want your audience to know, believe, or do—and then make sure that's what comes through in your message. Be simple and concrete.

- *Know your audience and what they want.* Target the go-to person—I call him the "get 'er done" guy—who can get you to your destination. And know what that person is going to want from you so you can talk about what's in it for him and why he might want to act on your message.

- *Develop a well-formulated approach.* My suggestion is to have a simple and direct sentence that's going to keep you on track. Don't get flowery. But do tease before you tell. That means you talk about the possibilities—for example, what the world might look like if you do this or what the project might look like if you do that—and *then* you tell your audience how to get there. The idea behind this tease-and-then-tell approach is to first paint a picture of the future and get your audience excited about that future so they're moved to take action.

PUTTING IT ALL TOGETHER IN A PRESENTATION

The presentation—with the featured speaker, the PowerPoint deck, and the audience around the conference room table—is a popular way to communicate in the business world, especially if you're making recommendations or selling something. But have you ever given a PowerPoint presentation that seemed to bomb? You weren't capturing anybody's attention, and you know that very few people were going to take any action after they left.

Dan Heath, coauthor of *Made to Stick*, offers some great tips to make sure that never happens.[5]

First of all, says Heath, be simple. To illustrate this idea, Heath tells the story about a trial lawyer who, after every trial, did a focus group with the jury to see what arguments worked. And here's the critical point the lawyer learned from all those focus groups over all those years: if you make ten arguments to the jury, no matter how good each one of those arguments is individually, they remember nothing by the time they get back to the jury room.

What does this mean for a presentation? Think of your colleagues as a jury, and be aware that if you say ten things to them, you say nothing to them. Let your main point shine through by getting rid of all the lesser points. Yes, it's hard to get rid of all those thoughtful secondary points on slide 16, but you need to be ruthless and cut back to the bone.

Second, show something. Heath says what you show doesn't even have to be on a slide at all. He talks about the president of a power tools company who was going to give a presentation to a major customer. The president had a beautiful PowerPoint deck about how great his tools were. But at the last minute, he decided to throw everything out. Instead, he simply put two drills on the table in front of the customer; one was his and one was the competitor's. And while the customer watched, the president took both drills apart and then put them back together to show how durable and elegantly designed his own drill was. The customer loved the demonstration, and the president got the account. Heath says this is the essence of what a presentation is all about; it's a way of bringing a little bit of reality into the room.

Finally, tease before you tell. Heath says that the number-one mistake that presenters make is assuming that their audience is going to be interested in what they have to say. If you want your audience to value your message, you've got to get them curious about it first.

THE 3CS APPROACH TO MESSAGE CRAFTING

Another way to approach this message-crafting business is through the 3Cs:

- Catch 'em
- Contain 'em
- Convince 'em

Here's an explanation of each of these steps.

CATCH 'EM: THE HOOK

You want someone to take action on your idea and you have a very short period of time to communicate, so start by setting the hook. Your first statement needs to advance your objective. It might be dramatic or it might be humorous; it might be personal or it might be anecdotal. It might even be a question. But in any case, it should be unexpected—something that you can hook somebody with, something that you can draw a person's attention to, something that might be memorable. Even your entire message can be a hook.

CONTAIN 'EM: THE CORE OF YOUR IDEA

Once you've caught your audience, you have to contain them with a core idea. Your core idea is expressed in language that is unambiguous in its intent yet is flexible in its implementation. You'll be constantly battling outside influences, so you will need to shave your message down to what I call the "commander's intent." This means the commander gives an order that's going to meet his ultimate objective. Then he leaves it to the platoon or a smaller entity to do the implementation. Good business leaders use the same approach; they are clear about the direction and objectives of the organization and what their intent is, and the team follows through with their own plan.

In the military, the intent, contained in an order or command, might be for soldiers to reach a certain hill or bridge. In business, it might be to close an account or finish a project on time. In communicating, strive to make the intent simple, concrete, and credible.

CONVINCE 'EM: THE CALL TO ACTION

So we've caught 'em, we've contained 'em, and now we have to convince 'em that they have to take action. But before you engage with someone, you should establish your MPVs: your minimum, primary, and visionary objectives.

A minimum objective might be grabbing someone's business card or making sure she heard your presentation. You simply cannot leave the room until your minimum objective is met. A primary objective is the specific result you want, such as arranging for a meeting, getting a person accepted onto a project, or being granted an extension on a deadline. A visionary objective is something that could be beyond your wildest dreams. If you're the manager on a tough project, maybe it's the client saying "Hey, can we double the size of the project?" My suggestion is to write all these objectives down—don't just keep them in your head. Writing your MPVs before any meeting forces you to be explicit in setting objectives.

When you do engage, you want to have a specific call to action with a specific deadline. If it seems as if you might not get that action, probe for information and then respond to that. You may have to go back and forth in an iterative process, but don't lose sight of your objectives, and don't ever be afraid to ask for a specific action. So many young leaders fail in this aspect of the communication; they do all the good legwork up front, but they don't have the nerve to ask for action. Don't lose your nerve.

MAKING IT WORK FACE TO FACE

Have you ever been talking with somebody at work or at home when that person said something like "It's not so much what you said. It's how you said it"? Me too. So I want to highlight unconscious communications in face-to-face engagements, whether one-to-one or one-to-many, and how you can deal with them.

Nick Morgan, the author of *Trust Me* (which was mentioned in chapter 2), is a big believer in the power of body language to communicate. A former speech writer extraordinaire and editor of the *Harvard Management Communication Letter* from 1998 to 2003, he's been tuned into this issue for years.

The idea is that your body posture will give certain messages—good, bad, or indifferent. And your facial expressions are going to say, "I'm happy; I want to be here" or "I'm miserable; I don't want to be here" or something in between.

According to Morgan, every communication is really two conversations. These consist of the words we use and our body language. When those two conversations are aligned, we can be effective communicators.

And when they're not aligned, says Morgan, people believe the body language every time. Let's say you're giving a speech and you're a little nervous. Your body sends out unconscious signals of danger, and the audience responds by sending unconscious danger signals back. The result is that they can't take in the words you're saying, so no communication happens.

Morgan writes about four steps to mastering this unconscious communication process. The first step is to be open because nothing can happen between two people unless they're open to each another. The second step is to connect; once people are open they can begin to relate to each other. The third step is to allow the passion for the content to come through. The fourth and last step is to listen because *every* communication is two-way. If you put these four steps together, you can be an authentic and charismatic communicator.[6]

I'd say Morgan is spot-on. I've personally seen poor unconscious communication undermine a leader's impact.

Just the other day, I met a company CEO whose handshake I still can't get out of my head. It was the classic "dead fish" handshake—no firmness, no energy, no eye contact, no effort to make a connection with me. And it was nothing like the classic American handshake that most of us are taught—take the person's hand firmly, shake it, and look him or her in the eye. It wasn't a cross-cultural issue because this CEO was born and raised in Detroit. After I met him, my only thought was "Whoa, I hope his work isn't as lackluster as his handshake." And it wasn't just the handshake; in general, his nonverbal communication conveyed a lack of confidence that will seriously inhibit his ability to inspire people.

His company is doing okay, and he's a smart man, but he needs to do better if he wants to lead his company effectively through the inevitable business ups and downs.

I have another client, a leader who's great one-on-one. But he struggles in a one-to-many forum like a podium speech or an all-hands meeting. During his one-on-one encounters, he is open and easily connects. His one-to-many opportunities happen only about four times a year, but he has to be ready to speak and get people excited about working for the company. During these public speaking events he struggles with finding passion for his topic and comes across as a preprogrammed monotone speaker.

MAKING IT WORK IN WRITING

What about situations where you can communicate only in writing? What makes the written word compelling?

Let's look at a couple of writing samples to see what works and what doesn't. These are about an upcoming get-together in a non-work setting, but they illustrate my points.

In the first sample, you've sent an e-mail that says, "I'd like to set up a 'dangers of drinking' campaign at school. Does anyone have any ideas? Let's have some coffee and cake." Do you think this will get the job done? Do you feel any emotion, any sense of urgency? Is it concrete, and does it call for a specific action? Not really.

Now here's the second sample. "I'm worried about all the teens at school who drink, and I'd like to set up a 'dangers of drinking' campaign. This is important to me, and I'm sure it is to you because it might keep your kids from drinking and even save their lives. I have index cards so we can write down suggestions while we have our cake and coffee." This message has a hook—a worry about teen drinking at school—and it connects to the readers' emotions as parents of teens. It's also concrete in describing the issue and quite specific about what action readers should take.

The question now is, Does this approach work in the workplace? Absolutely. As I said earlier, good communication techniques serve you equally well in business and your personal life.

Compelling communicators are well on their way to being great leaders. If you want to be one of them, remember this:

- *You need to make your idea stick.* To do that, use the SUCCES mnemonic as your guide.
- *You need to get your idea across in thirty seconds.* So use a hook, know your subject and your listener, and include a call to action.

Chapter 9

Plays Well with Others

The Tank, the Grenade, the Sniper. Are these characters in a war game? No. These are a few of the labels I use to describe folks with difficult behaviors that can wreak all kinds of havoc in the workplace. In this chapter, I introduce you to them all and explain how you can change the game—and get them to play well with others.

Someone else's behavior can poison a workplace situation, but your response as a leader can either exacerbate or calm that situation. You have to know how to assess an individual's behavior, the organizational environment in which that individual operates, and even your own responses to certain stimuli.

When you can do all that, you'll be able to apply certain proven strategies and techniques to manage difficult behaviors and ensure a more harmonious—and more productive—workplace.

WHAT MAKES PEOPLE DIFFICULT TO WORK WITH?

We've all met someone who is tough to work with. It might be the disgruntled employee who's coming into work late; the disheartened employee who seems to have given up on her career; the disingenuous supplier who doesn't seem to think that you're a key part of the program; the disinterested client who, even though he hired you, doesn't seem to be paying much attention to your project.

What makes people difficult to work with? Over the years, I've asked my workshop participants this question. They tend to say people are hard to work with if they are indecisive, they are working with a different agenda than you have, they have a hidden agenda, they are too complacent, they are passive-aggressive, they know it all, they whine constantly, they are always negative—the list goes on and on.

The trick is to figure out what to *do* about difficult behavior.

DON'T MAKE IT PERSONAL

Here's a crucial tip about dealing with a difficult person: deal with the behavior, not the person. Why? Because you're not going to be able to change the socioeconomic situation of that person. You're not going to be able to change the way that person looks or acts, the manner in which that person speaks, or the color of that person's hair. These are things that just *are*. What you want to focus in on is the person's behavior because this you can change.

Think of it this way: every difficult behavior represents a question—or even a few questions—that you didn't ask but need to. Why is the person acting this way? What are the underlying causes? What bothers me so much about that person's behavior? Is it impacting me, is it impacting the team, and is it impacting the organization? If there is an impact, then what strategy can I develop to stop the negative behavior?

Also consider this question: Is the behavior due to the "seeds" or the "soil"? The seeds would be the difficult-to-work-with person, and the soil would be the workplace environment in which the person operates.

The first step is to make sure that the person you're dealing with is in the right environment. In other words, start by checking the soil, which includes you and your behavior:

- *Is the troublesome person in the wrong job?* Many times, people get promoted into the wrong job. Their skills are a mismatch for the job, making it very difficult for them to live in concert with the attitudes, behaviors, and motivators that are natural for them. This creates a lot of tension in their lives, which can bring out poor behavior.

- *Does the job itself require the person to be difficult?* For example, has that job always been filled by somebody rather cranky? Was that last rather cranky person promoted quickly? If yes, then perhaps the new incumbent sees crankiness as a way to job success and is copying the behavior of the predecessor.

- *What are the group dynamics?* Often, fast-growing organizations have a bit of a leadership vacuum, and a strong-willed person can fill that vacuum and make life miserable for everybody else. Are roles and responsibilities clear, or has someone simply stepped in and filled the leadership gap in an unplanned and negative way?

- *Is the person's behavior a way of coping with a dysfunctional system?* This question is especially important if you're dealing with a large institution that may have little of the incentive or nimbleness needed to improve the soil. A dysfunctional system might be an expense or project reporting system that doesn't work well, a weak governance or product management process, or weak executive oversight, to name a few examples. Is the hard-to-work-with person dealing with this dysfunctional system in a way that's creating the negative behavior?

- *Is the organization somehow rewarding the difficult behavior?* Does this troublesome person keep getting promoted? When I first joined Boeing, I realized that it had an old-style command-and-control culture. Lots of little Napoleons were running around that organization because that's the kind of leadership style that was rewarded. But as you know, it's not the style I recommend if you want to manage the pace of change in today's business world and create a positive culture. But some large, longtime companies still find this a comfortable model, at least for the moment.

- *What makes this behavior specifically difficult for you?* Is it just a nuance of personality that rubs you the wrong way? Or is the behavior affecting the project, the team, the client, or some other key relationship in your industry and therefore needs to be addressed?

- *What effect has your response had on the person's difficult behavior?* For example, if you're action oriented and you run across a person who's on the passive side, what do you think will happen when you get more active? Typically, the other person will hunker down even more. If you get more intense, he will get more closed. In other words, you may be exacerbating the difficult behavior. So if you think you've dealt with the difficult behavior, consider how you've handled it. Have you dealt with it forcefully or negatively, not dealt with it at all, or dealt with it through an intermediary? And think about how the person has responded to the way you've dealt with his behavior.

Now that we've checked the soil—looking at environmental drivers of difficult behavior—let's begin to check the seeds, that is, the person who's demonstrating the difficult behavior. Do you really understand what motivates this particular hard-to-work-with person? Below I explain some assessment tools and concepts that can help you identify the personality drivers of difficult behavior.

TOOLS AND CONCEPTS TO HELP YOU

You can use a number of tools to understand how and why people operate the way they do. These are various types of behavior and attitude assessments. If you take one of these assessments, you can understand yourself better, and when results are shared across teams, they can help people understand one another better and work together more effectively. They can also help leaders lead with more impact and know how best to approach people and defuse difficult situations.

The Myers-Briggs Type Indicator (MBTI) has been around for a long time. It focuses on illuminating the way you think and deal with information internally and how you think about the world around you.

Another effective tool is the Core Values Index (CVI). It measures your combination of intrinsic core values to ascertain who you are and how you handle issues such as conflict.

You can also use StrengthsFinder 2.0. Developed by Tom Rath of the Gallup organization, it helps people begin to determine what natural talents they have; whether those talents are being applied properly; and, if not, how to begin to leverage them.

DISC, another popular tool, is often referred to as the universal language of human behavior. We use DISC a lot in my organization.

People often describe DISC as what it's not. It's not a measurement of emotional intelligence or personal intelligence or education or training. It's also not a measurement of your experience or your skills or your world-view.

What it does measure is *how* you do what you do. It's a measure of your own observable behaviors. These are presented in neutral language, meaning there are no good or bad behavioral styles in the DISC method; a behavior just is what it is, which is the reason I like this method so much. It allows you to communicate with other people more effectively and deal with their potentially challenging behaviors without getting personal.

You can use the tool to assess four dimensions of behavior: dominance, influence, steadiness, and compliance—DISC. Each dimension is described by a range of behaviors. Table 9.1 is an example of a DISC results page for an individual who's completed the DISC questionnaire.[1]

Dominance	Influence	Steadiness	Compliance
Demanding	Effusive	Phlegmatic	Evasive
Egocentric	Inspiring	Relaxed	Worrisome
		Resistant to change	Careful
Driving	Magnetic	Nondemonstrative	Dependent
Ambitious	Political		Cautious
Pioneering	Enthusiastic	Passive	Conventional
Strong-willed	Demonstrative		Exacting
Forceful	Persuasive	Patient	Neat
Determined	Warm		
Aggressive	Convincing	Possessive	Systematic
Competitive	Polished		Diplomatic
Decisive	Poised	Predictable	Accurate
Venturesome	Optimistic	Consistent	Tactful
		Deliberate	
Inquisitive	Trusting	Steady	Open-minded
Responsible	Sociable	Stable	Balanced judgment
Conservative	Reflective	Mobile	Firm
Calculating	Factual	Active	Independent
Cooperative	Calculating	Restless	Self-willed
Hesitant	Skeptical	Alert	Stubborn
Low-keyed		Variety-oriented	
Unsure	Logical	Demonstrative	Obstinate
Undemanding	Undemonstrative		
Cautious	Suspicious	Impatient	Opinionated
	Matter-of-fact	Pressure-oriented	Unsystematic
Mild	Incisive	Eager	Self-righteous
Agreeable		Flexible	Uninhibited
Modest	Pessimistic	Impulsive	Arbitrary
Peaceful	Moody	Impetuous	Unbending
Unobtrusive	Critical	Hypertense	Careless with details

Table 9.1 Sample DISC assessment

To evaluate this person's behavioral style, see what terms describe this individual in each of the four dimensions and whether they fall above or below the center line. The shaded areas indicate those behavior attributes most commonly exhibited. Here's a closer look at this example:

- *Dominance is how you respond to problems and challenges.* Someone who is conservative, calculating, cooperative, and hesitant—that is, someone whose behaviors fall below the line—would be called a "low D."

- *Influence is how you deal with others and move others to your point of view.* If you're a very "high I," you'd be effusive, inspiring, and magnetic, and someone who's a very "low I" would be pessimistic and moody. In our example, the "I" attributes are trusting and sociable.

- *Steadiness is how you respond to the pace of change.* For example, someone who's predictable, consistent, deliberate, steady, and stable would be a "high S"—someone you could see as being easy to work with and capable of handling change.

- *Compliance is how you respond to the rules and procedures that are set by others.* For instance, a person who happens to be systematic, dogmatic, accurate, and tactful is someone open to the rules and with balanced judgment.

I find that in our organization, the DISC system helps us communicate more clearly and deal more effectively with one another. It can be particularly helpful in dealing with difficult behaviors because if you know a colleague's style in terms of dominance, influence, steadiness, and compliance, you can map a communications game plan that accommodates those individual characteristics.

A corollary tool to the DISC tool, provided by the company TTI, is the Personal Interests, Attitudes, and Values tool (PIAV). The PIAV is an assessment that helps you understand the causes of conflict and begin to appreciate the viewpoint of others who might see life a little differently from you.

The core of the PIAV is the values piece. Values can be hidden motivators—the principles or standards by which you act. They are beliefs that you hold so strongly that they affect your behavior in the workplace.

The PIAV assesses the strength of your interests, attitudes, and values in six major categories. Here's what strength in each category suggests:

- *Traditional.* You generally hold core values close; these values are very important to you.
- *Theoretical.* You need to know how things work.
- *Utilitarian.* You are always interested in the return on investment; if you put something in, you want to know what you're going to get out.
- *Individualistic.* You want to know what's in it for you.
- *Aesthetic.* You appreciate the natural beauty of a situation.
- *Social.* You are interested in the social cause itself.

If you have your team take this assessment, you can gain insight into their values and what motivates their everyday actions. As a result, you can develop strategies to motivate each of them and reduce conflict among team members.

One key concept can help you get a grasp on people's behavior and how to deal with it. It's called "emotional intelligence." You can learn a lot about this concept from Daniel Goleman's book *Working with Emotional Intelligence.*

We all know what IQ is. The intelligence quotient has been studied and talked about for decades. Goleman's position is that success in the work world is not necessarily dependent on just IQ. While it's true that most CEOs, top salespeople, and successful scientists have a reasonably high IQs, Goleman points out that IQ can't be the only reason for their success because a lot of people with high IQs have not been successful in their work. He suggests that emotional intelligence can make the difference between success and failure. He defines it as the capacity for recognizing your own feelings and those of others.[2]

So that raises a question: How do you deal with people who have low emotional intelligence? These are people who often don't realize that their behavior is having a negative impact on the organization. They proceed blindly without seeing the implications. One simple technique you can try is to discuss the behavior with them. This is a challenge when a client's behavior is the problem, but having an open dialogue on how that person's behavior is impacting the performance of the organization may work.

The concept of emotional intelligence makes a lot of sense to me because in my life, I've met many people who are brilliant yet they have not cracked the code of success. But the more time I spent with them, the more I realized that something is missing in how they deal with people.

Now that you're armed with these key tools and concepts, the next step is to learn how to use them wisely.

YOU HAVE THE TOOLS, SO DON'T WING IT

Often, leaders wing it when dealing with challenging people. But remember, if someone is getting under your skin, then you may not be at your best when dealing with that person. You can use certain techniques to ensure you handle difficult situations as effectively as possible.

First, learn and master techniques for better self-control. Understand what your hot buttons are. For example, receiving criticism might create anxiety in you. You have to remind yourself that this is simply feedback. See it as an opportunity to become a better, more effective leader. A key step is self-awareness, but the critical success factor is self-control. It's not enough to perform a postmortem on your emotional outburst; you need to *avoid* the emotional outburst.

Create potential scenarios that could cause you to respond in a negative manner, and consider alternative responses. Understand the situation you must deal with and mentally rehearse your responses as often as possible. This may require you to role-play difficult situations with some of your cohorts to try out your self-control strategies.

Finally, ask for reminders from your peers that will let you know when you may be about to lose control. Arrange for them to signal you when you're being a little inflexible or when you're not seeing the situation clearly.

These are general approaches. You can fine-tune them once you have a better handle on the specific personality type you're dealing with.

LESS-THAN-LOVABLE PERSONALITY TYPES— AND WAYS TO DEAL WITH THEM

We've talked in general terms about difficult behavior and how you as a leader can manage it. Now let's meet ten difficult and distinct personality types that can inhabit the workplace. It pays to know which type you are dealing with so you can calibrate your approach appropriately.

WHINERS

Whiners feel helpless and overwhelmed by an unfair world. Their standard is perfection, and no one and nothing measures up to it. But misery loves company, so they bring their problems to you. Offering solutions makes you bad company, so their whining escalates.

Here's how to deal with Whiners:

- *Listen attentively to their complaints.* Even if you feel impatient, acknowledge what they're saying by paraphrasing it and checking your perception of how they feel about it because you want clarity.

- *Don't argue or apologize.* For the moment, you want to accept the situation from their point of view. At all costs, avoid a cycle of accusation, defense, reaccusation, defense, and so forth.

- *Try to move to a problem-solving mode.* Perhaps you can assign limited fact-finding tasks to them, or you can go out and find data that will help you reach a solution. In general, you want to be data driven but also supportive.
- *If all else fails, ask, "How do you want this discussion to end?"* This will put them in the position of taking ownership of their issues.

NO PEOPLE

Meet the Superman of difficult personalities. He is more deadly to morale than a speeding bullet, more powerful than hope, able to defeat big ideas with a single syllable. Disguised as a mild-mannered normal person, the No Person fights a never-ending battle for futility, hopelessness, and despair.

Here's how to deal with No People:

- *Be alert.* Don't be dragged down into their despair yourself.
- *Make optimistic but realistic statements about past successes in solving similar problems.* You need to paint a picture of the future that they can buy into.
- *Discuss a problem thoroughly before offering any solutions.* In other words, you don't want to solve the wrong problem in their point of view.
- *Deflate future negatives.* Raise questions yourself and note any negative events that might occur if solutions were implemented. Talk about the alternative and then discuss the positives and negatives that could come along. You're beating them to the punch on the negatives and minimizing their impact.
- *Be ready to take action on your own.* You may have to push through and announce your plans to take action without any equivocation. Make sure you're strong and forceful. You need to put No People on their heels and drive forward toward success.

NOTHING PEOPLE

These people give no verbal feedback and no nonverbal feedback—nothing. What else could you expect from Nothing People? Here's how to deal with Nothing People:

- *Set aside time for a conversation.* Get agreement on how much time you've set aside. (For example, "We have forty-five minutes; let's walk through this" or "We have only ten minutes; we can cover just a little bit.")

- *Rather than trying to interpret their silence, get them to open up.* Ask open-ended questions and try to see if they are thinking and responding.

- *Wait as calmly as you can for a response and then use follow-up questions.* Try again to see if they are thinking and responding.

- *Don't fill the silence with your own conversation.* Pregnant pauses are okay. Let them happen. Plan ahead for wait times and remain composed.

- *Eventually, offer some ideas and thoughts.* These ideas may land like a lead balloon, but try again to see if Nothing People are thinking and responding. Try to get a conversation going. It may take awhile.

- *If you get no response, comment on what's happening.* End your comment with open-ended questions. You want to plant seeds for more conversation so these people can at least begin to think about it.

- *Schedule a follow-up meeting if necessary.* Come back at a later time with a defined amount of time for conversation, and repeat the process outlined above.

MAYBE PEOPLE

These people procrastinate in the hope that a better choice will present itself. Sadly, with most decisions, there comes a point when it is too little, too late, and the decision makes itself. Life just passes them by.

Here's how to deal with Maybe People:

- *Be approachable.* Make it easy for them to tell you about the conflicts or reservations that prevent any kind of decision. If you come across as cold and unapproachable, they are never going to talk to you.

- *Listen for indirect words, hesitations, or omissions.* These may provide clues to problem areas. In other words, if you get the feeling that these people are not telling you the whole story, they're certainly not.

- *When you surface problems, help solve them.* These people may want to stall you, but help them examine the facts and reach a decision.

- *Watch for signs of abrupt anger or withdrawal from the conversation.* The situation may become too overwhelming for these people to actually make a decision.

- *Provide support after a decision is made.* These people are so uncomfortable making decisions that you have to keep giving them moral support.

YES PEOPLE

To please people and avoid confrontation, Yes People say yes without thinking the matter through. They react to the latest demands on their time by forgetting prior commitments, and they overcommit until they have no time for themselves. Then they can become resentful.

Here's how to deal with Yes People:

- *Try to surface the underlying facts and issues.*

- *Show that you value them as people.* Perhaps ask about their families, their hobbies, and maybe what they're wearing if it's appropriate.

- *Ask them what might interfere with your good working relationship.*
- *Compromise and negotiate.* Take this step if you sense conflict that you need to work on.
- *Be very careful to listen to hidden messages.* These people will engage in quips and teasing and "Of course I'll do that" kinds of comments. They just can't say no, but inside those yes responses might be clues that you can analyze and use to help these people.

THINK-THEY-KNOW-IT-ALLS

These people can't fool all the people all the time, but they can fool some of the people enough of the time, and enough of the people all the time—all for the sake of getting some attention.

Here's how to deal with Think-They-Know-It-Alls:

- *Assert your own perceptions of reality.* State the correct facts or any alternative positions and opinions as descriptively as possible.
- *Allow them to save face.* They've backed themselves into a corner, so give them an opportunity to get out of that corner.
- *Be ready with content to fill in conversation gaps.* Your statement of reality may be so different from their view of the situation that some gaps in conversation will occur.
- *Deal with them outside a team atmosphere.* Meet with them one-on-one if possible so you have the opportunity to address specific problematic behaviors.

KNOW-IT-ALLS

Seldom in doubt, Know-It-Alls have a low tolerance for correction and contradiction. If something goes wrong, however, Know-It-Alls will speak with the same authority about who is to blame—and it will be you!

Here's how to deal with Know-It-Alls:

- *Review the pertinent materials and check them for accuracy.* This includes all statements and all data.

- *Listen carefully and paraphrase their main points.*

- *Avoid making dogmatic statements that could put them off.* Also convey your appreciation for their knowledge.

- *Use questions to raise the problems.*

- *As a last resort, choose to subordinate yourself to avoid the static.* This may allow you to build a relationship of equality in the future.

GRENADES

The Grenade can be one of the most difficult personality types to deal with. After a brief period of calm, the Grenade explodes into unfocused ranting and raving about topics that have nothing to do with the present circumstances.

Here's how to deal with Grenades:

- *Try to slow down the situation.* You want to give these people time to run out of energy and regain self-control, if that's possible.

- *If necessary, interrupt their tantrums with a neutral phrase.* Try something like "Stop!" You don't want to comment on anything; you just want to put this show on hold for now.

- *If a breather is still needed, get some privacy.* Take them into the hallway or another room, and begin to lower the volume. You need some moments of calmness when you can address the root cause of the problem.

- *Take their comments seriously.* Grenades see themselves as serious people.

SNIPERS

Whether through rude comments, biting sarcasm, or a well-timed roll of the eyes, making you look foolish is the Sniper's specialty. Snipers can make you react very negatively.

Here's how to deal with Snipers:

- *Smoke them out.* Don't let social conventions stop you. You need to address the sniping immediately.

- *Provide an alternative to a direct contest.* Offer them a chance to meet you in your office or some other space that's not public.

- *Don't capitulate to their view of the situation.* Make sure you can talk about other points of view.

- *Try to solve any problems that are uncovered.* Something may be behind this sniping that you have to address—some underlying root cause.

- *Set up regular problem-solving meetings.* Many people snipe only when they're boiling over, so meeting gives you the opportunity to turn down the heat before it gets to the boiling point.

- *If two parties are sniping, stay out of the middle.* But do insist that it doesn't happen in front of you. Make it very clear that it's not appropriate behavior.

TANKS

As the name would imply, Tanks are confrontational, pointed, and angry. I'm sure you've dealt with Tanks before; sometimes we call them the "playground bullies."

Here's how to deal with Tanks:

- *Give them a little time to wind down.* They may not have enough ammunition to keep going very long.

- *Don't worry about being polite.* You need to get into the conversation any way you can.

- *Get their attention.* Try calling them by name or standing or sitting deliberately in their line of sight.

- *Try to have them sit, but maintain eye contact with them.* Show no sign of weakness.

- *State your own opinions forcefully.* Don't argue with what they're saying, try to cut them down to size, or make them feel insecure, but do be very clear, direct, and specific.

- *Be ready to be friendly.* When you attack the situation head-on, you have the opportunity to modify these people's behavior. This includes modeling the behavior you want to see.

DON'T JUST DO SOMETHING; SIT THERE: AN APPROACH TO CONFLICT RESOLUTION

A classic *Harvard Management Update* article showed that 42 percent of a manager's time was spent dealing with office conflict. So chances are, you'll have to deal with it sometime. Knowing when to intervene and when not to intervene is a bit of an art. You don't have to respond to every little hiccup in the office. Sometimes you can just sit there.[3]

Your decision to intervene should result from considered thought, not an emotional response to the conflict. You don't need to get involved every time you hear a rumor in the office. Remember the telecom commercial with the phrase "That's so forty-two seconds ago"? If you were off work for a few days, a whole life cycle of rumors started and stopped before you got back—without your attention. So you don't have to get involved in everything.

You *may* want to take specific action if resolution of the conflict can be used to improve the interactions (and perhaps the performance) of the group.

You *must* intervene, however, in the following cases:

- Someone—usually the more timid employee—is getting run over by another employee.

- An argument expands to include staff outside your team; then the conflict has become a cancer that's impacting other parts of the organization.

- The conflict becomes personal or it could have legal ramifications.

So how *do* you resolve conflict as a leader?

First, realize that what people demand is not necessarily what they need. Maybe someone is huffing and puffing and making all kinds of demands, but what that person really needs is to cool down.

Second, realize that your main job is not to assert your needs; it's to understand the other party. One of my favorite concepts about being involved in conflict is called "get up on the balcony." The idea is that when you're in the middle of an argument, a heated discussion, a tense negotiation, or other stressful interaction, you mentally jump out of your body, get up on the balcony, and look down on the situation to see where all the players are and who's doing what. If you do this, you can see all the dynamics of the interaction.

Let me share an example of this concept at work. A number of years ago, just after our division had joined Boeing, we all had to attend a meeting where the presiding Boeing executive gave a fifty-nine-slide presentation that lasted an hour. None of it related to what our division was doing, so we were unbelievably bored. Afterward, I made the mistake of agreeing to let my team respond to the presentation on our division's portal rather than filling out feedback cards on the presenter. Let's call him Roger. The three response choices were basically (1) We loved Roger, (2) We thought Roger was terrific, and (3) Roger was spectacular. However, there was also a place to write your own feedback. Of course, being part of an open and transparent company prior to acquisition, we welcomed feedback on our portal, and that's where my staff ripped Roger to shreds.

Shortly afterward, Roger called me out at a big all-hands meeting. I still clearly remember mentally getting up on the balcony and looking down at the situation and thinking, "He's out of line, but I can't defend myself. He's just uncomfortable with the feedback. Maybe I should have handled things differently, but it was an honest mistake." So I wasn't thrilled with his angry outburst, but by getting up on the balcony, I didn't lose control and respond negatively to Roger.

If you're dealing with a conflict within your team, remember that your job is to first understand the other parties and get above the fray. If you don't, you'll become emotional and you won't stand a chance of giving sound advice.

The third tip for conflict resolution is to concentrate on common interests, not differences. Keep focused on the best interest of the organization—for example, how we can get the job done and when the next deliverable is due.

BACK TO BASICS: A BROAD FRAMEWORK FOR MANAGING DIFFICULT BEHAVIOR

To close this chapter, let's pull back and look at some strategies that can broadly apply to every difficult situation:

- *Get everything out in the open.* Ask your team members to evaluate their actions. Consider using a checklist of positive and negative behaviors and asking members to identify which of those they need to develop, which of those they need to minimize, and which of those they may need to eliminate. The idea is to address negative behaviors *before* they lead to conflict in the workplace.

- *Agree on the ground rules for communication.* Ask the members of your team to adopt simple rules such as no personal insults and no negative statements.

- *Act promptly and frequently.* When something negative does happen, you need to interrupt the behavior quickly and then frequently follow up to support the new behaviors you want to see. Your constant feedback, coaching, and problem solving will be critical.

As a next generation leader, you want to shift the focus from blaming people to solving problems. This creates a healthier organization. You must also learn to transform difficult behaviors into opportunities for continued organizational growth and perhaps even nurture the personal growth of your teammates.

Chapter 10

Every Moment Counts

How many ways does your organization connect with customers? I'd venture to say it's too many to count. You can connect through an office visit, the delivery of a work product, a proposal, an executive lunch, a website, a brochure, an invoice, and the list goes on.

Your goal should be to make each of these connections a positive customer experience. That's a tall order because the digital age has given us endless ways to connect. Nevertheless, you need to understand how to evaluate your customers' experiences with your organization and use that understanding to nurture customer loyalty and advocacy.

Research shows that doing so can have a direct impact on the financial performance of your organization, which translates to a better financial picture for you too. Isn't this a great incentive to make every moment with your customer count?

PIONEERING RESEARCH FROM IBM

Every way you connect with a customer can be meaningful. This is not a new concept. In fact, in 2006, IBM did an incredible amount of research on its customer relationships. The company identified six separate ways it connected with customers—at a branch office, by phone, on the web, via mobile device, through a kiosk or ATM, and at an event—and then looked at how customers' feelings might vary in each situation.[1]

IBM also tried to tease out customers' feelings about its various products, services, and communications. The company looked specifically at whether customers felt positive or negative about core products or services, about the quality and ease of use of these products and services, and about ancillary services or features that might be available. IBM also tried to get a sense of how customers felt about its company brand and if price and value were issues that might drive them to continue to buy from IBM.

IBM took the research further by also looking at two aspects of the customer experience. One was tactile, which refers to objective measurements such as speed, availability, and price. The other was emotive, which describes how a person feels about an interaction, expressed in terms such as trust, dignity, and empathy.

IBM found that where the customer has a low personal investment, emotive factors are 50 percent less important than the tactile ones. This might be the case, for example, when someone's opening a checking account; in this scenario, a customer wants to get the task done quickly, have the service readily available, and have the price be right.[2]

However, if the customer has a high personal investment—think of an experience such as the purchase of a new car—then emotive factors are 40 percent more important than tactile ones.[3]

This means that if you're selling a product or service that a customer is personally invested in purchasing, you need to make a personal emotional connection if you want to create a positive and successful customer experience. But if the personal investment is low, you have to address the tactile factors if you want to make the experience good for the customer.

Creating and maintaining strong customer relationships is a cumulative process. You have to win customers through an endless array of what I call "customer touch points." These are, quite simply, all the interactions between your customers and your company over the course of the relationships. A touch point can occur via an ad, a website, a salesperson, a store, or an office. And each is important because customers form perceptions of your organization and your brand based on these accumulated touch points.

As you read about the different ways to identify and improve customer touch points, think about whether you have a system in place to back the kind of customer service you want to deliver. For example, my former business associate's son has feet that are two different sizes. Nordstrom was the only place they could buy him shoes when he was a child because the store would break up two pairs of shoes and sell a single shoe in each size. That's great customer service, of course. But think about what it took for the store to deliver on my business associate's expectation. The store had to have a supply management operation that could work with vendors to get them to take back all the single shoes that weren't purchased, it had to train salespeople to understand that this practice of breaking up a pair of shoes was allowed, and it had to have an inventory management system that could deal with the situation. In short, the store had to institutionalize its flexible approach to customer service.

Another example of institutionalized high-quality customer service came to me courtesy of a client who frequented Four Seasons Hotels. First, he stayed at the Tokyo Four Seasons, where one night the family called down for a snack. The hotel sent up the requested order, which included a hot chocolate chip cookie for their young son. During checkout, our client commented on how much his son enjoyed the cookie. Later on in their trip, they stayed at another Four Seasons—this one in Los Angeles—and the night they arrived there, a hot chocolate chip cookie was delivered to their boy, even though they hadn't requested it. Now that's a business with a well-developed system in place to back up its customer service practices.

TOUCHING THE BOTTOM LINE

Why should we care so much about these customer touch points? Here are a few reasons:

- Business growth comes only from an increase in purchase rates. People have to keep buying more of your products and services.

- Purchases are decisions customers make based on their needs and expectations. They're buying something from you because they need something, and they expect something as a result of their relationship with you.

- If you're relevant to your customer—or even better, already a positive and necessary part of your customer's experience—then you have a chance to drive more growth.

Think about some successful businesses and brands. Apple is working on being relevant in your life, with elegant products designed to meet your needs. The experiences most people have in an Apple retail store are very positive. If you're a coffee lover, Starbucks may be relevant in your life. You may find the coffee drinks delicious and the touch point of the retail operations welcoming. As for me, I love Dunkin' Donuts, so I have a Dunkin' Donuts locator on my phone and I normally purchase my ten-ounce cream-only coffee at the drive-through.

These businesses understand the goals of managing customer touch points: to improve market share, sales, and customer and employee loyalty and advocacy.

If you don't believe that improving the customer experience can help you achieve these goals, consider the fast facts below:[4]

- Even in a down economy, the customer experience is a high priority for consumers, with 60 percent often or always paying more for a better experience.

- Eighty-one percent of companies with strong capabilities and competencies for delivering excellent customer experiences are outperforming their competition. In other words, great work always counts.

- The top three reasons that companies invest in customer experience management are to improve customer retention, improve customer satisfaction, and improve cross-selling and up-selling.

- Dissatisfied consumers will tell between nine and fifteen people about their experience. About 13 percent of dissatisfied customers will tell more than twenty people about their experience. Bad news travels fast, so try to prevent it from happening in the first place.

- Eighty-six percent of consumers quit doing business with a company because of a bad customer experience, and that's up from 59 percent just a few years ago.

- For every customer who complains, twenty-six other customers have remained silent. So the one who actually shares a complaint with you is giving you a gift.

- It takes twelve positive service experiences to make up for one negative experience.

- Ninety-one percent of unhappy customers will not willingly do business with your organization again.

- Happy customers who get their issues resolved tell four to six people about their experience. So even when you do make a mistake, you need to resolve it and be very clear with the customer about the steps you took to clear up that mistake.

- Attracting a new customer costs five times as much as keeping an existing one. That may not surprise you, but it's important to keep in mind. Taking care of your existing customers is business-critical.

- Seventy-six percent of companies motivate employees to treat customers fairly, and 62 percent provide effective tools and training to gain trust with their customers.

These facts all tell you that you have to pay attention to customer service. To reinforce this, let me share a cautionary tale with you; it shows the consequences of *not* paying enough attention to a customer.

When the firm I worked for was acquired by a larger firm, we lost our ability to set up and manage contracts at a local level. This function was shifted to our new firm's headquarters on the West Coast—our operations were based in the East—and at first it seemed like a small issue. But over time, it caused delays in our responses to contractual changes, invoices, and return payments. Even though we were still providing a good work product, we weren't as responsive in terms of how we managed contracts. From our customers' standpoint, it was a big deal and we lost work because of it. Our customers wanted to be able to call somebody in our firm and say, "Can we amend this part of the contract?" and have it taken care of right away. But with the new arrangement, we were dealing with a three-hour time difference, not to mention a large contracts bureaucracy at headquarters that could not turn on a dime like we had before.

So remember how crucial *each and every* touch point can be.

THE CHANGING WORLD OF CUSTOMER SERVICE

In the predigital age, touch points were finite and every one of them was analog—that is, it was an in-person, by-phone, or in-the-store experience. If you needed a screwdriver, you walked down Main Street to the hardware store and bought one. You may have even known the store owner, the store clerk who helped you find the right screwdriver, and the person who rang up your purchase on the cash register. Perhaps you called ahead to see if that screwdriver was in stock, but even that touch point was analog.

Then came the digital age, with its multiple connected touch points. The old analog ways and the newer digital ways of connecting were blended. You might go to a restaurant (analog) but pay for it with a coupon you pulled off the web (digital).

My son worked at a Jimmy John's sandwich shop during his summer vacation, and it provides a great example of the challenge of blending the analog and the digital. You can tweet ahead with your order at Jimmy John's, but that doesn't necessarily mean your order will be ready when you get there. If the worker asks the customer, "When did you tweet ahead?" the customer might respond, "I was just around the corner when I did it." The tweeting capability raises the customer's expectation of instant gratification beyond the shop's ability to meet it.

Sometimes everything works together, of course. I had a positive experience recently with Comcast. I did a lot of troubleshooting with the company about my cable service through an online chat session. Then I went to the store to pick up a new cable box that would solve my problems. On the whole, it was a very good blended digital-analog experience.

And while we still have these blended experiences, we've already entered what might be called a "postdigital age," characterized by infinite touch points. In this era, the digital and analog lines are *really* blurred, and the volume of social connections has expanded exponentially. You might be running a business and driving growth through a Twitter account with thousands of followers.

But with infinite possibilities for connection comes the fragmentation of your customer relationships. You're connecting with people, but you don't always know what their intent is, what their actions are, and what their satisfaction level is. This presents its own set of challenges.

UNEXPECTED TOUCH POINTS

Lest you think customer service has already gotten complicated enough, consider customer touch points that many times go unnoticed or unconsidered—but shouldn't.

Here's one example that the CFO of a client company shared with me. This CFO prides himself on his appearance. He is a handsome guy, always looks sharp, wears cufflinks and ties—you get the picture. His firm was being audited, and the auditor who visited his office could have been on the cover of *Mr. Frumpy Magazine*. The CFO recognized the clash of styles, so the next time the auditor came into the office, the CFO made sure it was a dress-down day for him. He felt it would make for a better relationship with the auditor.

Another overlooked area of touch points for service businesses is the work product. Some companies focus on engagement management and service-delivery methodology. Project kickoffs always happen a certain way, deliverables always happen a certain way, and so on. But in other companies, the whole process is a little scattered, leaving the customer saying, "I didn't know this step would happen next" or "A proposal? Nobody said anything about a formal proposal coming my way."

So pay attention to how you deliver your work products. Consider how many aspects of the work touch your customer; these include reference management, field intelligence, proposals, statements of work, workflow management, requests for information, and quotes. Are you handling these with consistency and with an eye to how the customer experiences each? Also consider the way you may be segmenting customers. Are you segmenting them hierarchically so you can target and deal with certain executives in a certain way? And what about billing? Will the customer find your billing practices flexible?

In addition, think about every aspect of how you present your brand. You'd be amazed at what constitutes a marketing touch point. For example, I had lunch the other day with a company CEO who is an incredibly energetic person. He's got an "upward and onward" attitude that shines through. He was my first contact with the company, so for me, this very positive touch point set my expectations for the company as a whole.

Other marketing touch points include your company name, logo, or trademark; your website and e-mails; printed materials; reports and sales communications; company announcements and other releases or interactions with the media; corporate or product advertising; corporate sponsorships; promotional items; and even your office presence.

Another business area rife with touch points is recruiting. As Lauren Weber noted in a 2012 *Wall Street Journal* article, on average, 8 percent of job candidates came away from their application experience with enough anger and resentment toward the company that it affected their relationship as a customer of the firm. That's a big deal.[5] And consider what might happen if all those angry, resentful candidates talk about their experience with just one other person? The percentage of those with a negative perception of your company can grow.

Weber went on to cite an example of a large retailer that hires 5,000 people a year and receives 100 résumés per job opening. The company therefore rejects up to 495,000 candidates per year. If 8 percent of those rejected candidates plus one close associate each resent the firm at the end of the hiring process, the retailer may lose 79,200 current or potential customers. If each customer spends an average of $100 a year with the retailer, the annual revenue loss would be $7.92 million.[6]

Some companies manage the candidate experience well. At one professional services company, for example, the HR recruiting manager is considered an executive of the company. So when he's recruiting candidates, they experience it as an overture from a C-suite person, so it has a real impact. That company's closure rate for candidates is very high. Think about what your company might do to enhance the candidate experience because you can't afford to alienate 8 percent—or more—of your customer base.

Specific touch points with prospective employees include the following:

- *Your company's recruiting website or its presence on third-party career sites.* These are places where you should strive to make a great first impression.

- *Phone calls and e-mails to candidates.* Make sure you are building a good relationship with candidates as quickly as possible.

- *Employee referral programs.* Your team needs to not only understand why your company is a great place to work but also know how to explain this to potential candidates.

- *Polls and surveys.* Make sure these are not experienced as intrusions.

- *Career fairs and events.* In chapter 1, I shared the story of how I decided to ramp up recruiting for my company to better compete with a neighboring firm that was hosting an extravaganza of a career fair. Events with the right style and tone can make an impression.

- *Career newsletters.* You could, for example, present tips on growing a career while also talking about your company.

- *User forums.* A number of years ago, I had a technology client who put together an early Java-users group. The group didn't have anything to do with the company per se, but all the meetings were hosted at the company's offices. The benefit for the company? It had thirty to forty Java programmers walking into its building once a month. There's no downside to that. Plus, it raised the company's profile among this talent pool.

- *Open houses and job fairs.* These can work especially well if you have an interesting office space to show off and if you've advertised the events well enough to ensure a good turnout.

- *Campus information sessions.* These work great if you are trying to hire young talent. As always, your goal is to get candidates to think good thoughts about the company.

- *Meet-ups.* You could sponsor or organize a meeting, or a series of regularly held meetings, for people who share a particular interest and have connected with each other through a social-networking website.

- *Intern and co-op programs.* These not only are a great way to identify talented individuals at a young age and get them into your talent pipeline, but also give them a useful work experience that will predispose them to think about—and talk about—your company in positive terms.

BUILDING CUSTOMER ADVOCACY

By now, I hope you can see that there are not only an infinite *number* of touch points in our postdigital age but also an immense *range* of customer touch points. Together these touch points become your customers' experience. The better that experience, the better your business will do: a positive customer experience leads to better relationships, which build market share and can lead to customer loyalty and may create customer advocacy.

In fact, customer advocacy should be your end goal in managing customer touch points. In other words, job candidates should say nice things about the recruiting process, clients should say positive things about your deliverables, current and prospective clients should say good things about your proposals, and so on.

Customer advocacy on its own doesn't necessarily drive sales increases, but it gives you a chance to close in on sales because the customer will be predisposed to favor you. You must ensure that everyone on your team understands that every moment—every interaction with a client, no matter how routine—counts. Each

touch point can help build a positive story about your company—
or a negative one.

Overcoming a negative story can be difficult. To illustrate, let
me share a story about a firm that ran into trouble with one of its
government-agency clients. It had staffed the agency's project with
people who signed contracts agreeing to work on-site for the agency
exclusively, in a secure facility where everyone had to swipe an ID
badge to record entry and exit times each day. One of these people
was a junior engineer who recorded eight hours on his timesheet
each workday. After he'd been working there for eighteen months,
someone compared his timesheet data to the agency's badging system and discovered that he'd actually been on-site for only seven
and one-half hours each day. This was, to put it bluntly, fraud. As if
this wasn't bad enough, it created a negative customer touch point.
Can you imagine having the conversation with the client about
eighteen months of regular overcharges?

Consider how this negative story about the company then
floated throughout the industry. It raised all kinds of concerns:
maybe this company didn't have the infrastructure to support basic
payroll operations; maybe it lacked good governance practices;
maybe it didn't have the necessary security policies and timesheet
policies in place; maybe it was not as smart a company as everyone
thought it was!

All those repercussions were due to just one junior engineer
who wanted to pick up an extra half-hour of pay each day.

Now let's talk about a positive story that provides some lessons on how to assess and improve the customer experience. It's
the story of Enterprise Rent-A-Car. In 1994, the company was
coming off a decade of huge growth, but CEO Andy Taylor and
his corporate management team were getting the sense, through
calls and letters from customers and word of mouth, that customer
service was falling short in terms of both quality and consistency.
On the other hand, operating managers—the folks who were

primarily responsible for the company's impressive growth—felt that the company did not have a customer service problem or that the problem was insignificant.

To assess the scope of the problem, Enterprise developed a survey tool to measure customer satisfaction levels. To get operating managers on board, the company involved them in the tool's development and also persuaded them to take ownership of the measurement process. At first, the survey data was reported at only the regional or group level, but as interest in the data grew, the company began reporting at even the local level. The assessment process had begun with mail surveys but switched to phone surveys to increase the timeliness of the feedback.

By 1996, Enterprise had timely, actionable data that it could use to hold individual branches and managers accountable for the quality and consistency of the service they delivered. Everybody in the company generally understood the data and accepted the measurements of customer experience as valid. Enterprise even included the information in monthly operating reports, right next to the net profit numbers that determine a manager's pay so it would be taken seriously. Nevertheless, the company had shown only modest improvements in customer service.

So that same year, the company required operating managers to achieve customer satisfaction levels that were average or above average before they could qualify for promotion. The result was a significant improvement in customer service. By the late 1990s, the number of completely satisfied customers had risen by 10 percent. In addition, the gap between the top-performing and the bottom-performing scores had narrowed, which meant service was more consistent. These results are what Enterprise had been aiming for when the survey program was introduced.[7]

Some great lessons were learned from the customer service experiment at Enterprise:

- *Good managers don't always know what and where they need to improve.* The insights on where and how to improve customer service came only after the company had collected data for a number of years.

- *Complete customer satisfaction does not mean perfection.* Plenty of customers had experienced problems but remained satisfied if the problems were handled well.

- *Action on a problem requires both a sense of urgency and a willingness to align performance and rewards.* Once operating managers realized that they couldn't be promoted without delivering on customer service, the desired business results followed.

Think about how you can apply these lessons to your own team or organization. Figure 10.1 provides a framework for mapping each of your customer touch points so that you don't miss any when you are formulating a plan for assessing and improving the customer experience. For example,

- Note that the map is divided into two zones: digital touch points and physical touch points. Does your team or your company fit in the digital zone, the physical zone, or both?

- On what aspect of the customer experience do you have the most impact? If you're in sales, you probably fall in the awareness and consideration areas of the map's horizontal bar. If your work revolves around product delivery, you fall in the purchase and service areas. And everyone is involved in loyalty at some point.

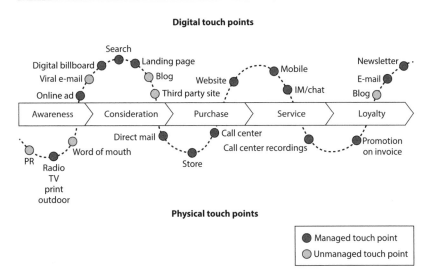

Figure 10.1 Mapping customer touch points

Now that you've learned a lot of about customer touch points, here is a slightly provocative question to consider: Do touch points apply only to external customers? According to Doug Conant, the answer is no. Conant, a thought leader on employee engagement, suggests that, as next generation leaders, we should view each of our interactions as a touch point and an opportunity to engage people who work in every part of the company.[8]

Growth comes only from increased purchase rates, customers make purchase decisions based on their needs and expectations, and if you are relevant, then you have the opportunity to make more sales. So make every moment with each customer count.

Chapter 11

The Connected Workplace

Leaders struggle when they try to go it alone. Leaders flourish when they build strong relationships and leverage them.

The reason is that leaders are human, and human relationships have worked the same way from the very beginning. From tribes to communities, from families to businesses, when we surround ourselves with other competent people we can rely on, we create a force multiplier that enhances our lives, our societies, and the prosperity of our businesses.

That's why it's so important to know how to build your network of relationships and nurture those relationships. If anything, they are more important than ever in today's hyperconnected world.

If you can master the myriad ways we can create connections and nurture personal relationships, you'll be an effective leader in the workplace.

"NO MAN IS AN ISLAND"

Chances are, at some point in your business career you've been told, "It's not what you know; it's who you know." I'm not going to argue that point, but I would suggest that to be successful in the workplace, you need to get to know people and work well with them.

Early in my own career, I noticed that some people paid a lot of attention to their connections. They seemed to know everybody, and they knew how to use that knowledge. They knew where the next hot product was or the next job opportunity or the next contract. Some people are naturally great at this. Others are not. Whatever your natural inclinations, you can get better at making connections and making them work for you in the workplace—and you should.

This point hit home with me when I witnessed the experience of a colleague. He had worked for the government for many years as a senior executive, but when he left the government, he realized he had no network. This hurt him because he wanted to be a consultant. In addition, he could be blunt; he wasn't afraid to break a few eggs to make an omelet, and if you worked with him, you were either a big fan or you didn't like him at all. He'd attempt to get a consulting job and the prospective clients would say either "We'd love to have you on board to help us do this" or "We don't want to have anything to do with you." So he realized that, at age sixty-two, he had to start developing his network if he wanted to grow his business.

Why is connecting with others in the workplace essential? It is a basic aspect of being human. We want to connect for security or comfort—to feel a sense of belonging. We might also feel the pull of shared values, ideas, or interests. And I've already talked about the shared vision, goals, and purpose that can bring people together in a business setting.

Think about all the different settings where you can connect. We do it in our families, of course. But we also belong to bands, tribes, clans, fraternities, clubs, teams, cliques, gangs, and organizations. We join for a sense of belonging we feel from our affiliation with the group.

The Elizabethan-era poet John Donne wrote about this human connection quite eloquently centuries ago in his poem "For Whom the Bell Tolls." Its most famous lines read:

> No man is an island,
> Entire of itself.

Each is a piece of the continent.
A part of the main.

And isn't this even truer today? We live in an incredibly inter-connected world, with hardly a place left where someone would be totally off the grid.

OPERATING IN TODAY'S HYPERCONNECTED WORKPLACE

The ways you can connect with colleagues are numerous and var-ied. But networking is not all about connecting with as many people as you can. It's more about the relevancy of your connec-tions. Suppose, for example, you have one hundred connections on LinkedIn. Your one hundred connections may be way more power-ful than the eight hundred connections of the person sitting next to you—*if* your criterion for connecting is the relevancy of those connections to your business and your career.

David Meerman Scott, a prominent thinker in online market-ing, can provide some perspective on this issue. He says you should develop relationships with connections if you want to grow your business. Your list of connections will therefore be smaller because you are focusing on developing an intimacy with your custom-ers. For example, you might have a customer newsletter that goes to two hundred or three hundred people, but they are the *right* two hundred or three hundred people. Another organization might ship a newsletter to ten thousand people, but only two hundred people in that distribution list may be relevant to the business.[1]

In fact, you should think of your network as your force mul-tiplier—the factor that dramatically increases the effectiveness of your effort. Your primary focus is to deliver your product or service to your customers. If your connections are tapped into the right knowledge—for example, knowledge of the marketplace, the cur-rent technology, or the next big thing—then you can tap into that as well. You don't have to know everything yourself. Your connections give you a lot of leverage in your effort to stay on top of what customers need and want.

As you grow in your responsibilities as a leader, the depth and relevance of your network will help you achieve success on a number of fronts. Some great reasons to nurture your connections are to find great people, find fulfilling work, match abilities to needs, be part of the next big thing, and know which way the wind is blowing.

Three digital tools that you should definitely consider using in building connections are LinkedIn, which I've already mentioned, Facebook, and Google+.

Facebook is the main social-networking platform on the planet. It has more than a billion active users. You can use it to create an online profile; add other users as "friends"; and exchange messages, post updates and photos, and view updates from others. You can also use Facebook to set up common-interest groups and organize groups by workplace, school, or other affiliations.

I think most professional people tend to split their social media time between Facebook and LinkedIn, and it's an approach you might want to consider as well.

Of the two, LinkedIn is the more business-oriented networking site. Used mainly for professional networking, it has 396 million registered users in more than two hundred countries and territories.[2] You can use this platform to create a professional profile and connect to other professionals. You can also use LinkedIn to find jobs, people, and business opportunities; publish blogs; or promote products or services. Employers can even list jobs and search for candidates on LinkedIn. Sales professionals can use their Sales Navigator product to search for prospective customers. Overall, it's a great way for businesspeople to get connected and stay connected.

Google+ has an incredible array of features, and Google seems to be adding more on a daily basis. It's a "social layer" that overlays and enhances many of Google's online properties, such as YouTube, and it now has a user base of more than 540 million. With Google+, you can group people into "circles" based on types of relationships rather than simply have "friends." But keep in mind that the majority of Google+ users are under age thirty-five; this is a factor to consider as you begin to leverage it for your business relationships. Still, it's a powerful tool, and I'm really interested to see how Google+ does over time.

NURTURING YOUR BUSINESS RELATIONSHIPS

How do you nurture your business relationships—that is, strengthen your existing relationships and increase the number of connections you have? I recommend a multipronged approach.

First, make connecting part of your everyday work life. This includes incorporating a practice that author Stephen Covey recommends: make deposits before you ask for withdrawals. By this, he means that you have to invest the time in a person before you can ask that person for a favor.[3]

Also, use every means available to connect. Here are some common options:

- Make a phone call or send a text or an e-mail.
- Meet for a meal or drinks or engage in another social activity.
- Join a professional association. Whether you're in technology, the building trades, communications, or another field, you'll find a professional association that fits your business.
- Write personal letters, notes, and cards. Whenever I've done this, it's had a huge impact on my professional relationships. That handwritten communication takes a little time, but it goes a long, long way.

Have you heard of Refer.com (formerly 22Touch)? This is a digital tool that helps you stay in touch and maintain relationships with the people who can provide you with business referrals. You can add contacts from various places—for example, you can import them from LinkedIn, Salesforce, or Outlook—and then classify them by order of importance. Once you're set up, Refer.com automatically schedules touches based on how much interaction you'd like to have. Each day, you'll be prompted on whom to contact and how to contact them. I'm sure other tools are available, but this one provides a pretty easy way to deepen relationships.

Now that I've highlighted several ways you can nurture business relationships, I want to remind you to pay it forward. Take some of these suggestions back to your team. If they're a junior team, they may not be thinking enough about their business relationships. They haven't had the time and experience to see how investing in these relationships pays off. Your job is to make sure they start paying attention to connections. Plus, as your team builds their connections, you can leverage these connections to expand your own reach.

It's all about taking action rather than sitting back and hoping for the best. Here are some specific ways you can leverage connections for business success:

- Spend more time on connections.
- Get to know your connections' connections.
- Consider reconnecting with old or weak connections.
- Find new recruits through your connections.
- Find the next big opportunity by discussing the future with your connections.
- Schedule coffee or lunch with a connection.

Of course, taking action is not as easy as it sounds. You do have to pick and choose: you can't have lunch with everybody all the time. And from a business standpoint, the decision about how to spend your valuable time should be based on return on investment, as cold as that may sound. After all, you and your connections are developing relationships with the purpose of helping one another in business.

Clearly, this is a long game, so let's review the tools you can use to *stay connected* over time. I've grouped them into three categories so it will be easy for you to remember them:

- *Old media.* This category is all about one-on-one communication—using the phone, e-mail, or notes to connect personally.

- *New media.* This category involves one-to-many communication. New media include LinkedIn, Google+, Facebook, and Twitter, as well as blogs, online chats, and more. You need to use these media to increase the number and eventually the relevancy of your network.

- *Mama media.* This category is more personal. It includes coffee meet-ups, lunches, dinners, visits to a customer site or a prospect site, meetings, social gatherings, industry events, and functions anywhere else where you can network and develop additional relationships and connections.

Yes, it takes effort to get connected and stay connected. But why not embrace the effort? After all, it's part of being human. And it really will lead to more business success for you.

Chapter 12

Stepping It Up

W ho's responsible for business development in your organization? Is it your marketing and sales staff? Of course. But the responsibility for growing the business doesn't end with them.

If you're a division vice president, a chief operating officer, a project leader, or a task manager—even if you're just getting started in your leadership odyssey—you too have a role to play in how your business grows. You need to build on your current skill set to extend your business operations and expand your customer footprint. And you need to make sure your team does their part in extending and expanding the business as well. In doing so, you will serve your career and your company well for years to come.

The key is to figure out what's working and then work it more. This is called "stepping it up."

NURTURING BUSINESS DEVELOPMENT SKILLS

If your business is going to fulfill its potential, you need to raise the business development skills of everybody in the organization. That doesn't mean you should turn everyone into a salesperson. People specialize for a reason, and you want the software developer and the engineer to focus on what they do best. However, you and *everyone* on your team must learn how to interact with customers and grow customer relationships.

It's not enough to know that developing new business is a goal. You have to embrace the idea that it's a natural extension of doing business and that it's part of everyone's normal routine.

This is something that must be preached and practiced until it becomes part of your culture. If you invest little in getting out the message, you'll get little back in return. But if you get the message out frequently and help each team member understand clearly both the expectation and what to do about it, you're going to see a huge return on investment. And when everyone begins to interact with customers effectively and see and act on opportunities, you will begin to experience a phenomenon called "organic business growth."

AIMING FOR ORGANIC BUSINESS GROWTH

Here's the organic-growth concept in a nutshell: You have a base of work, and you're going to find a way for that to grow incrementally from year to year. For example, if you have a three-person project generating $500,000 in annual revenue, then the objective would be to add value for your customer and become a four-person project generating more revenue in the next year and then more in the years after that so that the business keeps expanding.

In contrast, what I call "acquisitive growth" is more about bidding on projects, submitting proposals to chase specific opportunities, or even acquiring programs or whole companies, with a longer-term strategic agenda. It can often be more of a sales effort, akin to making cold calls and knocking on doors. Although it's a viable way to grow a business, you'll find that unless you're leading a marketing group, your staff will not be comfortable with this approach, so it's not a practical way to nurture business growth through your team. I recommend organic growth because it will grow the business in a way that will feel most natural to your team.

Figure 12.1 contrasts the value and pace of growth from the two approaches. The "present curve" is based on organic growth, which builds up gradually over time. The "future curve" is based on acquisitive growth, which is often a much riskier approach with lumpy results. The present curve is about increasing operational efficiencies, and the future curve is about major change initiatives. Each milestone on the present curve represents an incremental gain, while each milestone on the future curve represents a major, and potentially risky, initiative. As you and your team step up your business growth activities, I encourage you to stay on the present curve—that is, pursue organic growth in a way that makes that curve as steep as possible.

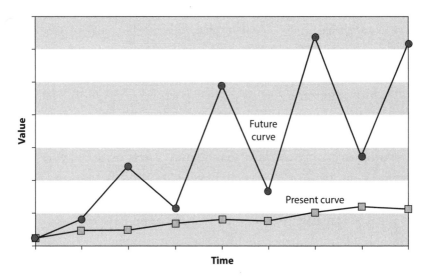

Figure 12.1 Present and future curves

Organic growth has three elements: expansion, extension, and rollover. You may not have heard these terms in this context before, so let's go over what each one means.

Expansion is developing new work with an existing customer. This can be in the form of a pilot implementation, the follow-on development effort from an initial study, or a new functionality added to an existing system. The goal is to *expand* your footprint in the existing customer space. Expansion could also be bringing a new service or product offering to that customer.

Extension is bringing the same or similar service offerings to a new but related customer (such as a customer of a customer), sometimes referred to as a "tangential" customer. Your high-quality service delivery supports this effort because the work you are currently performing can be referenced to a prospective customer. Serving a tangential customer makes sense, and it's easy to get your team comfortable with it because you are not selling; you are just making contact with the next logical prospect. The goal is to *extend* your market-segment footprint.

The concept of market segment is important to discuss here. A market segment is a set of customers with similar functionality and profiles. I like to use the image of a bowling lane to help people picture a market segment. When we're using a particular bowling lane, we're dealing with one market segment. If we're in telecommunications, that's one bowling lane, but if we decide over time that we need to be in food services, that's a different bowling lane. Entering that different lane may require a less organic approach, typically on the future curve, that would not involve you and your operational team but rather a marketing and sales initiative targeting that new market. Sometimes, you can jump bowling lanes—for example, if your current client moves to a new market segment—but in general, you're going to stay in that one bowling lane, in that one related market segment. This way, even though you're going somewhere that's new, you're taking with you something you're really knowledgeable about, which is a key to stable growth.

What we're going to stay away from in our bowling alley is "new new"—that is, a new service offering in a new segment. This situation generally brings too much risk because it's harder to manage. We don't have the customer relationships, we don't have the intimacy with the staff, and we don't know all the ins and outs of this new service offering.

The final concept of organic growth is rollover, which is developing a new and longer contract with an existing customer. The goal is to *roll over* current development or short-term work into longer-term work to create a continual revenue stream for the company—all supported by an ongoing customer relationship. This work can sometimes be maintenance or support types of service offerings. Or it may be work that used to be a little risky or avant-garde—maybe a pilot program or prototype—but is now less risky and is being turned into a cash cow. The goal in rollover work is to create a recurring revenue stream based on your prior excellent service or product delivery.

BUILDING THE BUSINESS: GREAT SERVICE IS THE FOUNDATION

Extending and expanding your business is almost impossible if you're not currently delivering great services. But satisfying the customer has inherent challenges. David Maister, coauthor of *The Trusted Advisor*, makes this point well. Maister's First Law of Service is this: satisfaction = perception – expectation. But his second point about service is that neither perception nor expectation necessarily reflects reality. He says that both are experiential states of mind. This is frighteningly true.[1]

So our challenge as managers, leaders, consultants, or team leaders is to manage the substance of what we do for our clients—in other words, the reality—and to manage the client's perceptions and expectations of what we do.

For example, I used to work with a programmer who wrote all the code for one of the very first secure databases. He had a doctorate from Princeton in computer science—the sharpest guy in town. He was on the project team I led. (I'd like to say I managed him, but he was one of those people who refused to be managed.) Even though his work was stellar, our client never realized this because this programmer never said the right thing in front of the client. Although the programmer was brilliant and the client needed him and we needed him, we always had a hard time managing the client's perception of this man's contributions.

This story reminds me of how a project team is sometimes compared to an orchestra. You have great musicians who must work together to create great music. Even if you have the best cellist in the world, if he can't work within the construct of the orchestra, the music will sound terrible. Likewise, the quality work of one computer science expert doesn't necessarily look like quality *service* to the client.

Even if clients perceive your service as great, you still have to keep reminding them of how good you are because, quite frankly, they can forget. Let me remind you of the client service mantra I mentioned in chapter 7, which borrows from the professional presenters' approach ("Tell them what you're going to tell them, tell them, and then tell them what you told them"). In client service, the mantra is "Tell them what you're going to do for them, do it, and then tell them what you did for them. And then tell them what you did for them, and then tell them what you did for them." That's because the harsh truth is that the value of services rendered *after* they've been rendered drops precipitously over time. Think about it: how thrilled were you to pay $180 an hour to the plumber right when the leak was finally stopped? But then you had to write the check for two hours of service and you had to listen to your spouse say you could have fixed it yourself, and pretty soon the value of the service rendered seems to be lower.

The same devaluation happens with professional services. A great book called *Selling the Invisible*, by Harry Beckwith, talks about how a service, unlike a product, is not something you can touch and hold and take home—hence the concept of selling the invisible.[2] Over time, if you don't keep reminding clients of your value, your perceived value to them drops and undermines your potential for organic growth through these clients. So make sure your team understands the mantra and knows to remind the customer "We have done a good job for you; we have done a good job for you; we have done a good job for you. We have value."

You also need to understand and be aware of the three stages of marketing to existing clients. You can't leave out any of these stages. The first is to make the client predisposed to use your company again. The second is to increase your company's capabilities to serve the client. The third is to find and pursue the next engagement with an existing client.

MAKING YOUR CLIENTS WANT TO USE YOUR SERVICES AGAIN

The first stage of marketing to existing clients is making the client predisposed to using you again, and a big part of this is going that extra mile on current engagements. Does your team believe in doing that, or are they the eight-hour-workday crowd? Maybe you need to have a conversation with team members along the lines of "What would the extra mile look like for this client? Would it be something to make the client's life easier or more productive? Would it save the client money? Would it save time?"

To answer these questions, your team must understand the customer's world. You can't be expected to know everything about a certain field, but you've got to know enough to be able to have a conversation about what your company can do to serve that customer base. Perhaps you can do some consulting with the customer yourself to model the right behavior for your team.

However you approach this stage, you need to teach your team how to save the day, give the extra time or service, and provide the added value. It can really pay off. For example, a number of years ago, my company was a subcontractor to a larger company on some of its clients' projects. In these subcontracting relationships, we were always on time and we always gave the larger company exactly what it needed. At one point, our teams were at a joint meeting about a new client proposal when the client's program manager got up and said to his people, "I want you to do it just like Marty's company does it." It was a great testimonial from a customer, and we got it because we always went the extra mile.

Of course, going the extra mile is sometimes a little tricky if it entails going out of scope on a project. If you're asked to do something that wasn't in the original contract, how do you manage the request in a way that's going to be profitable for you and valuable to the client?

My suggestion on managing out-of-scope work is to break it down into issues of time, money, and functionality and then find out how the client wants to prioritize these. I learned this lesson the hard way. We had a client that wanted to launch a product, called the "Wage and Information Retrieval System," by the time horse-racing season started. We made the mistake of thinking that functionality, not the timing, was the most important aspect. "It has to work!" we said. Why? Because we were staffed by detail-oriented engineers who thought that functionality was of critical importance. But to the client, the most important requirement was that the product had to be done by horse-racing season, even if it didn't have as much functionality. We didn't grasp this, so we didn't manage the timing requirement. We should have tried harder to understand the client's priorities. Doing so is part of going the extra mile.

Another aspect of making the client predisposed to using your services again is to find ways to increase the amount of client contacts. This is a big part of your job as a leader. How often are you on the job site, having discussions with the client? You should ask lots of questions regarding the current project and then follow up with correspondence letting the client know you heard and understood what she said and are taking action focused on meeting her needs.

It's good to have a plan on how you'll engage the client. I would suggest writing down your MPVs—that is, your minimum, primary, and visionary objectives—prior to any face-to-face engagement. This will give you a tool for managing the process. A minimum objective might be to touch base with the client. At the other end of the spectrum is the visionary objective—the absolutely best outcome of a client contact. It might, for example, be a profitable twofold expansion of a project. It's important to be prepared for that eventuality.

As you expand your client contacts, you will be building a relationship that may further predispose the client to use your services. Here are some tips on how to do this:

- Have at least an annual planning session with the client.
- Talk about the business or the industry rather than the technical nuances of the project.
- Establish trust and rapport; be genuinely interested in the person.
- Know something about the client; talk in terms of the client's interests.
- Employ a servant leadership mentality: get your client promoted.

A fascinating book that will give you more ideas on how to expand client contacts is *Involving Customers in New Service Development*. It discusses involving the client in your whole service offering methodology and development.[3] For example, if your service offering is a certain way to do help desk management, then you would engage the client in the entire process of developing the help desk function. In this kind of engagement with clients, you'll develop a thirst for understanding the business, will be positioned to do things right the first time, and can establish credibility early.

INCREASING YOUR CAPABILITIES TO SERVE CURRENT CLIENTS

When you're talking to your team about developing their capabilities to serve your current clients, focus on these four areas:

- *The client's industry.* Do you know what's going on in the industry? Do you know what's going on in the client's market segment? For example, are you keeping up with technology developments in that market segment?
- *The client's business.* Do you know what's happening with the client's business? Is the company doing well, or are there areas of concern?
- *The client's organization.* Do you know how the various parts of the organization fit together? When you work for that client, where is that work going to be deployed, and who within the organization is going to see it?
- *The client as a person.* Do you know the client's educational background or where and how he spends most of his leisure time? This is where the earlier tips on building relationships come in.

Now suppose you have enhanced your capabilities to serve a specific client and you've made sure the client is predisposed to using your services. Even so, to successfully market to the client, you still have one more stage to manage: identifying, pursuing, and ultimately landing the next engagement with that client.

FINDING AND PURSUING THE NEXT ENGAGEMENT WITH A CURRENT CLIENT

To manage this last stage of marketing to existing clients, you and your team must engage in a number of activities.

First, understand that creating opportunities to demonstrate initiative and competence to the client is absolutely critical.

Second, dig up intelligence on a new client need, assemble evidence of that new need, and create awareness of the new need in the client. If you wait for the client's request for proposal to come out, it's probably too late because your competitors see it at the same time. You've lost your advantage. So make sure you're regularly having conversations with your staff about what clients need. But also explore what they may just want; I've heard stories about clients who would jump on a new technology no matter what. Once you have identified a possible need, assemble evidence of it and then have a conversation about it with the client.

Third, find sponsors, friends, and coaches in the client organization. Who's a gatekeeper? Who knows what's going on inside the organization? It might be a chief of staff or an administrative assistant who manages calendars and knows how to get you in to see people. It may be someone who knows about the budgets; follow the money to see where the next engagement might be likely and see if you can be in a position to influence the decision.

Finally, ask for the new engagement—at the right time, of course. I find that the toughest part of the marketing process for many people is to ask for the order. If you personally struggle with taking that step, it's fine, as long as somebody on your team is able to go in and ask for that new engagement.

BOWLING FOR BUSINESS: EXTENDING AND EXPANDING MARKET PRESENCE

We know that we can *expand* our business through an existing customer with new service offerings, and we can *extend* our business with an existing service offering to a new, tangential customer. Now let's bring these ideas together in the form of the "bowling pin model" of business development. It's a great supplement to any account management strategy you might have.

Before we get into the details of the model, however, here's a primer on a few concepts that it uses: a whole service offering, a segment, and the technology adoption life cycle.

A whole service offering encompasses more than, for example, just a specific technology. It also includes the skills and competencies of your company. You have people who are trained to use certain intellectual-property tools, products, templates, and best practices. It's rather like having a full tool box. You are also leveraging market-segment knowledge, successful past performances, and subject-matter expertise. You deliver it all using a specific service-delivery methodology.

A segment refers to market segments that you're either in now or could logically enter.

The technology adoption life cycle, first identified in research done many years ago, shows the timing for the adoption or acceptance of a new product or innovation by defined adopter groups: innovators, early adopters, early majority, late majority, and laggards. Each group has its own demographic and psychological characteristics; for example, early adopters tend to be younger and more educated. You can see where these groups fall in the life cycle by looking at figure 12.2.

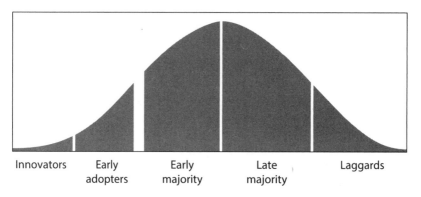

| Innovators | Early adopters | Early majority | Late majority | Laggards |

Figure 12.2 Moore technology adoption life cycle

The figure title includes Geoffrey Moore's last name because in the book *Crossing the Chasm*, Moore introduced a variation of the original life cycle, which inspired the concept of the extension-expansion approach to business development. Moore said that many new products get only the early adopters. But if you can't get into the early majority marketplace, then you fall into what he termed "the chasm." He said you have to have a beachhead in the early majority for your product to have a chance to stick there and to avoid the chasm.[4]

Now let's see how these concepts play out in the bowling pin model. Figure 12.3 brings the bowling pin analogy to life.

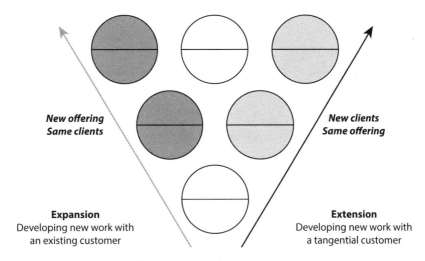

Figure 12.3 Bowling pin exercise

The process starts with the lead bowling pin at the bottom of the figure. That's our existing client base and our beachhead, so to speak, for expanding or extending our market presence.

Note that the lead bowling pin has two halves: the top half represents the whole product or whole solution you're offering, and the bottom half represents the customer. You can decide to leverage either of these. Here's how it works.

To the left side of the pin—the expansion side—we keep the client the same and we have a new whole service offering, that is, a solution for that client. You take this approach, called "word-of-mouth leverage," if you've thought about how you've made the client predisposed to using you, you've analyzed your capabilities, and you've identified a new need that you can address with your new

offering. It's pretty easy, frankly, to bring new offerings to existing clients. You know the players and you have relationships with
them.

It's a little harder to take what you've done for other clients—
that is, the same whole service offering—to a new client. This is
the extension approach illustrated on the right side of the figure.
If you're going to use this approach, you need to be very thoughtful about what client to target. My suggestion is that you focus on
a tangential prospective customer. Maybe it's a client of a client,
a former client that moved into a new space, or somebody that
you met at a conference serving your field. Tangential prospective
customers may have similar needs and are generally open to learning more about your product or service because you've already had
success with a similar customer.

As you can see, you can work on either side of the bowling
pin model—the extension or the expansion side—depending on
your analysis of your capabilities and market opportunities at the
time. Once you've decided on an overall approach, you should create a plan for approaching the next prospective customer. If you're
uncomfortable taking your offering to the prospective customer
yourself, discuss the plan with your manager or sales representative,
and make sure that that person is engaging the customer with the
plan that you developed.

The bowling pin model provides a useful way to approach business development as part of the organic growth concept. The idea
is to build on the current good work that you've done. You don't
have to ask your engineers, field service technicians, or software
developers to make cold sales calls. You need to find the next logical
bowling pin and knock it down—that is, win that new business.

Chapter 13

Go Make a Difference

Change is a constant, so every organization needs strong leaders to create a vision or establish a direction and then align the organization with that direction. Organizations that can develop leaders prepared to deal with and lead change will prosper. Those that can't will rise and fall with market trends and eventually fade away.

The journey toward developing the next generation of leaders is divided into three segments. The first is a deep reflection on and the development of yourself and your team. An honest assessment of your personal skills, competencies, strengths, behavioral and communication styles, and desire to serve can be uncomfortable, but it's necessary in your leadership development journey.

The second segment in the journey is the leadership of the client or other stakeholder, such as an employee of your company or even a vendor. Your knowledge of your stakeholders and your ability to serve them is an essential element of leadership. Without your leadership, your teams won't respond, your projects won't grow, your customers won't be happy, and your market share won't expand.

The final segment of the leadership development journey involves your ability to connect with your team and clients and move them toward your vision. The world is filled with brilliant technicians—people who can write elegant software, design an engineering masterpiece, compose the perfect contract, or craft a masterful proposal. But society is woefully short of leaders who can paint a picture of the future and move people to take actions that make that picture become a reality.

YOUR ROLE

This is where you can make a difference. You have the opportunity to take the leadership reins of your project, your team, your territory, your division, or your company. However, many organizations tend to develop their employees at only two times—shortly after onboarding and shortly before a huge promotion.

Imagine a barbell for a moment. Developing technical skills early in one's career is a positive step, but leadership development can't stop there. The focus on technical skills has the effect of creating skilled technicians on one side of the barbell with very little understanding of why they are doing things. They are great at the what and how—but missing out on the why.

Many companies try to make up for this lack of leadership depth by force-feeding leadership training to a chosen few. This has the effect of taking great senior technical skills out of the marketplace and turning excellent technicians into average managers. At other companies, thoughtful leadership programs are offered, but they are few and far between. This attempt at grooming the leadership skills of more senior staff represents the other side of the barbell.

Project leaders, field service managers, team leads, and even divisional leaders with profit-and-loss responsibilities find themselves unprepared to lead. These managers are often responsible for succeeding on projects that make or break the businesses they work for. However, they must lead their critical projects with fewer direct reports, less money, less time, and little training or professional development.

To reverse this barbell effect, organizations need to support and develop leaders in the middle so they can learn to become a new breed of leader—a leader who understands the why and not just the what and how. In other words, organizations must find a way to develop leadership depth to match today's real-life management challenges.

LEARNING TO LEAD

Developing your leadership skills is a lifelong endeavor that you should view as a joy rather than a burden. The journey is the goal. Embracing leadership development as a lifelong process means even after you've been long retired, you will still enjoy the intellectual stimulation of thinking about how to make your world a better place.

Trial and error is an inherent part of leadership development. Your specific work assignments and job experiences will shape your thoughts on how to lead colleagues, customers, and markets. You will experience ups and downs. View each of these challenges as a way to progress in your professional development.

You will also have the opportunity to observe leaders around you. As you observe, learn from both great examples of leadership and bad examples. Consider the poor responses you observe and determine how you might respond differently in these situations. Look for role models in the areas of communication, demeanor, style, and content. Think about how these role models developed their skills, knowledge, and competencies. Don't limit yourself to observing leaders only in the workplace because often you'll find examples of excellent leadership in other settings.

Finally, you should seek formal education on the subject of leadership. As an adult learner, consider using the "get it, know it, use it" approach:

- *Get it.* Access and spend time on the content. Read books, watch videos, review white papers, talk with your mentors, and listen to lectures, stories, and anecdotes about leadership. Look for every possible method to learn the basic tenets of leadership.

- *Know it.* Begin to internalize the content and make a con-science decision that you will be a change leader. Understand your current work situation and commit to applying your new knowledge to it. The objective is to make a difference and make change stick.

- *Use it.* Actively practice what you've learned. Once you've made the investment of time and energy in the content and you've made the emotional commitment to make a differ-ence, use what you've learned in a real work situation.

FIRST CHANGE YOURSELF

When you grow as a leader, you will be able to change lives. You may also change the world. And the best way to start is by chang-ing yourself.

The following words were written on the tomb of an Anglican bishop in the crypts of Westminster Abbey by an unknown author:

> When I was young and free and my imagination had no limits, I dreamed of changing the world. As I grew older and wiser, I discovered the world would not change, so I shortened my sights somewhat and decided to change only my country. But, it too seemed immovable. As I grew into my twilight years, in one last desperate attempt, I settled for changing only family, those closest to me, but alas, they would have none of it. Now as I lie on my deathbed, I sud-denly realize, if I had only changed myself first, then by example I would perhaps have changed my family. From their inspiration and encouragement I would then have been able to better my country and, who knows, I may have even changed the world.[1]

Notes

CHAPTER 1

1. Niccoló Machiavelli, *The Prince* (New York: Alfred A. Knopf, 1992), 1515.
2. Thomas L. Friedman, *The World Is Flat: A Brief History of the Twenty-First Century* (New York: Macmillan, 2005), 92.
3. Thomas L. Freidman, "The World Is Flat" (presentation, IBM Think Forum, New York, September 29, 2011).
4. John P. Kotter, *Leading Change* (Boston: Harvard Business School Press, 1996), 33–145.
5. Robert McKinney, Michele McMahon, and Peter Walsh, *Danger in the Middle: Why Midlevel Managers Aren't Ready to Lead* (Boston: Harvard Business Publishing, 2013).
6. Ibid., 3.
7. Ibid., 6.
8. Bill Toler, interview by author, Annapolis, MD, March 18, 2010.
9. Winston Lord, "Episode 15: China—Interview with Ambassador Winston Lord," George Washington University, National Security Archive, January 24, 1999, http://nsarchive .gwu.edu/coldwar/interviews/episode-15/lord1.html.

CHAPTER 2

1. Nick Morgan, *Trust Me: Four Steps to Authenticity and Charisma* (San Francisco: Jossey-Bass, 2008), 18–19.
2. David H. Maister, Charles H. Green, and Robert M. Galford, "The Rules of Romance: Relationship Building," chap. 5 in *The Trusted Advisor* (New York: Free Press, 2000).
3. Ken Blanchard, Donald Carew, and Eunice Parisi-Carew, *The One Minute Manager Builds High Performing Teams* (New York: William Morrow, 1991), 31–64.
4. Robert Coram, *Boyd: The Fighter Pilot Who Changed the Art of War* (New York: Little, Brown, 2002), 327.

CHAPTER 3

1. Matthew Kelly, "The Dilemma," in *The Dream Manager* (New York: Hyperion, 2007), 1–5.
2. Rodd Wagner and James K. Harter, *12: The Elements of Great Managing* (New York: Gallup Press, 2006), xv.
3. George Gallup Jr., ed., *The Gallup Poll 1999* (Wilmington, DE: Scholarly Resources, 1999), 248–249.
4. James M. Kouzes and Barry Z. Posner, *The Leadership Challenge*, 3rd ed. (San Francisco: Jossey-Bass, 2002), 21.
5. John P. Kotter, "Leadership Qualities, Characteristics of Followers, and Situational Factors," chap. 3 in *The Leadership Factor* (New York: Free Press, 1988).
6. Kouzes and Posner, *The Leadership Challenge*, 8.

CHAPTER 4

1. Daniel H. Pink, *Drive: The Surprising Truth about What Motivates Us* (New York: Riverhead Books, 2009), 27.
2. Towers Watson, *2012 Global Workforce Study*, 9.

3. Chicago Booth/Kellogg School, "Financial Trust Index: Wave 21," accessed December 10, 2015, http://financialtrustindex .org/resultswave21.htm.

4. Ken Blanchard, John P. Carlos, and Alan Randolph, *The 3 Keys to Empowerment: Release the Power within People for Astonishing Results* (San Francisco: Berrett-Koehler, 2001), 5.

5. Pricewaterhouse Coopers, *Global Growth and Innovation Survey* (London: Pricewaterhouse Coopers, 1999).

6. Stephen R. Covey, *Principle-Centered Leadership* (New York: Free Press, 1992), 86–93.

7. Max DePree, *Leadership Is an Art* (New York: Doubleday, 1989), 20.

8. Peter W. Schutz, "Administrative Roles in Leadership" (workshop, Rapid Systems Solutions annual retreat, Queenstown, MD, October 1995).

CHAPTER 5

1. Stephen Denning, *The Leader's Guide to Storytelling: Mastering the Art and Discipline of Business Narrative* (New York: John Wiley & Sons, 2011), 12.

2. *Merriam-Webster.com*, s.v. "engaged," accessed December 10, 2015, http://www.merriam-webster.com/dictionary/engaged.

3. Amy Adkins, "Majority of U.S. Employees Not Engaged Despite Gains in 2014," January 28, 2015, http://www.gallup .com/poll/181289/majority-employees-not-engaged-despite -gains-2014.aspx.

4. G. K. Chesterton, *The Everlasting Man* (New York: Dodd, Mead, 1925).

5. Terry Waghorn, "How Employee Engagement Turned Around Campbell's," *Forbes*, June 23, 2009.

6. Ibid.

7. Douglas R. Conant and Mette Norgaard, *Touchpoints: Creating Powerful Leadership Connections in the Smallest of Moments* (San Francisco: Jossey-Bass, 2011), 126.
8. Wagner and Harter, *12*, xv.
9. Mark Ehrnstein, interview by author, Annapolis, MD, February 11, 2010.

CHAPTER 6

1. David H. Maister, Charles H. Green, and Robert M. Galford, *The Trusted Advisor* (New York: Free Press, 2000).
2. Jeffrey M. Jones, "In U.S., Confidence in Police Lowest in 22 Years," June 19, 2015, http://www.gallup.com/poll/183704/confidence-police-lowest-years.aspx.
3. *Merriam-Webster.com*, s.v. "trust," accessed December 10, 2015, http://www.merriam-webster.com/dictionary/trust.
4. Stephen M. R. Covey and Rebecca R. Merrill, *The Speed of Trust: The One Thing That Changes Everything* (New York: Simon and Schuster, 2008), 125.
5. Ibid., 12.
6. Matthew Kelly, "The Best Way to Live," chap. 1 in *Off Balance: Getting Beyond the Work-Life Balance Myth to Personal and Professional Satisfaction* (New York: Hudson Street Press, 2011).

CHAPTER 7

1. Robert K. Greenleaf, *The Servant as Leader* (Indianapolis: Robert K. Greenleaf Center for Servant-Leadership, 1970), 7.

CHAPTER 8

1. Chip Heath and Dan Heath, "Introduction," in *Made to Stick: Why Some Ideas Survive and Others Die* (New York: Random House, 2007).

2. Philip Martin, "General Things about Good Stories," pt. 1 in *How to Write Your Best Story: Advice for Writers on Spinning an Enchanting Tale* (Milwaukee: Crickhollow Books, 2011).

3. Johnson & Johnson, "Our Credo Values," accessed December 13, 2015, http://www.jnj.com/about-jnj/jnj-credo.

4. ExxonMobil, "Our Guiding Principles," accessed December 13, 2015, http://corporate.exxonmobil.com/en/company/about-us/guiding-principles/our-guiding-principles.

5. Dan Heath, "Made to Stick: Presentations That Stick—How Do You Avoid That Bullet-Riddled PowerPoint Presentation That Everybody Loves to Hate? Here Are Three Ways," *Fast Company*, April 7, 2010, http://www.fastcompany.com/1603022/made-stick-presentations-stick.

6. Morgan, *Trust Me*.

CHAPTER 9

1. Ron Bonnstetter, "15 Things That Set TTI SI Behaviors Assessments Apart," TTI Success Insights, accessed December 13, 2015, http://www.ttisuccessinsights.com/articles_papers/18.

2. Daniel Goleman, *Working with Emotional Intelligence* (New York: Bantam Books, 1998), 317.

3. David Whitemyer, "Don't Just Do Something—Sit There," *Harvard Management Update*, December 1, 2002, 3.

CHAPTER 10

1. IBM Global Services, "Advocacy in the Customer Focused Enterprise" (Somers, NY: IBM Corporation, 2006), http:// www-935.ibm.com/services/us/gbs/bus/pdf/ibv-advocacy -ge510-6276-03f.pdf.
2. Ibid.
3. Ibid.
4. Mary Shulzhenko, "20 Shocking Customer Service Facts and Stats," *Provide Support Blog*, February 18, 2015, http://www .providesupport.com/blog/20-shocking-customer-service-facts -and-statistics/.
5. Lauren Weber, Angry Job Applicants Can Hurt Bottom Line, *Wall Street Journal*, March 13, 2012, http://www.wsj.com /articles/SB10001424052702303717304577279473549339082.
6. Ibid.
7. Andy Taylor, "Driving Customer Satisfaction," *Harvard Business Review*, July 2002, http://www.hbr.org/2002/07 /driving-customer-satisfaction.
8. Conant and Norgaard, *Touchpoints*.

CHAPTER 11

1. David Meerman Scott, *The New Rules of Sales and Service: How to Use Agile Selling, Real-Time Customer Engagement, Big Data, Content, and Storytelling to Grow Your Business* (New York: Wiley, 2014), 202–211.
2. Statista, "Numbers of LinkedIn Members from 1st Quarter 2009 to 3rd Quarter 2015," accessed December 18, 2015, http://www.statista.com/statistics/274050/quarterly-numbers -of-linkedin-members/.
3. Stephen R. Covey, *The 7 Habits of Highly Effective People: Powerful Lessons in Personal Change*, 25th anniv. ed. (New York: Simon and Schuster, 2013), 188.

CHAPTER 12

1. David H. Maister, "The Psychology of Waiting Lines," Columbia University, 1995, last modified 2005, http://www .columbia.edu/~ww2040/4615S13/Psychology_of_Waiting _Lines.pdf.

2. Harry Beckwith, "Marketing Is Not a Department," in *Selling the Invisible: A Field Guide to Modern Marketing* (New York: Grand Central, 2012), 33–54.

3. Bo Edvardsson et al., eds., *Involving Customers in New Service Development* (London: Imperial College Press, 2006), 6.

4. Geoffrey A. Moore, *Crossing the Chasm: Marketing and Selling High-Tech Products to Mainstream Customers*, rev. ed. (New York: Harper Business, 1999), 9.

CHAPTER 13

1. Marshall Goldsmith and Laurence Lyons, *Coaching for Leadership: The Practice of Leadership Coaching from the World's Greatest Coaches*, 2nd ed. (San Francisco: Pfeiffer, 2006), 60.

Index

message delivery (*continued*)
  See also communication
middle managers, 4–5
mind-sets/beliefs, 47, 95–98
minimum objectives, 131–132
misalignment, organizational, 20
mission, 33, 43
"mission to Mars" pitch, 127
mistakes
  allowing some, 53
  in presentations, 129
modeling behavior, 33, 35
models, business. *See* business/operating
  models
Moore, Geoffrey, 192–193
Moore technology adoption life cycle,
  192–193
Morgan, Nick, 11–12, 132
motivation
  common performance goals for, 40
  lack of, 48
  recruitment example, 7
  sources of, 143, 144
MPV (minimum, primary, and visionary)
  objectives, 131–132
Myers-Briggs Type Indicator (MBTI),
  141

N
Napoleon, 8
need(s)
  anticipating, 60–61
  versus demands, 154
  of stakeholders, 113–116
needs-based relationships, 13, 94
negative attitudes and behaviors, 147, 155
negative experiences, 158
networks/networking, 167, 173–178, 179
new service offerings, 184, 193
No People (personality type), 147
Nordstrom, 159
Norgaard, Mette, 79
Northwestern University, 49
not-for-profit groups, financial models,
  70–71
Nothing People (personality type), 148

O
Off Balance (Kelly), 97–98
O'Neill, Denise, 120
*One Minute Manager Builds High
  Performing Teams, The* (Blanchard), 17
one-over-ones tool, 15
online connections, 175, 176–177
OODA Loop, 19
openness in communication, 133, 134
operating model. *See* business/operating
  models
operational parameters, 70–71
opportunities, for employees, 77–78
organic business growth, 182–185, 194
organizational culture
  alignment of people and purpose
    through, 43–46
  assessing your, 58
  culture fit of candidates, 81, 82
  empowerment, 56–57
  equity, 20
  high-performance, 78
  inclusiveness, 67–68
  ownership (*see* culture of ownership)
  performance, 37
  purposeful, 45–46
  trust, 48–49
organizational growth. *See* business devel-
  opment/growth
organizational structures, 20
orientation stage of team evolution, 18
out-of-scope work, 188
Overseeing team development, 16–19
  See also COACH tools
ownership
  building (*see* COACH tools; TRUST)
  of company brand, 67–68
  culture of (*see* culture of ownership)
  mind-set of, 47
  of one's issues, 147
  trust for building, 50–56

P
Parisi-Carew, Eunice, *The One Minute
  Manager Builds High Performing
  Teams,* 17–19
Pariveda Solutions, 72–73
passion, 23, 133, 134

Services Offered

Martin O'Neill:
Speaker, Consultant, Trainer, Executive Coach

Martin O'Neill offers a range of services that help organizations develop their next generation of leaders.

TRAINING

Your long-term business success depends on your next generation of leaders. So developing those leaders needs to be one of the primary responsibilities of your organization. Next Generation Leaders is a twelve-course online program designed for team leaders, project and program managers, new and future leaders, division managers, and others who have an interest in growing their leadership skills. To learn more about developing leaders in your organization, visit www.martinoneill.net/training.

KEYNOTE SPEECHES

Marty can speak to your organization on the following topics:

How Your Business Will Prosper When Everyone Acts Like an Owner. Imagine if everyone in your business knew how the company operated and entrepreneurial employees were rewarded for being stewards of the business. That's the power of an internal franchise. In the current business environment, a great product or service is no longer enough. Today, success or failure is determined by how well an organization can align, inspire, and mobilize people around its strategy.

Building Business Value—How to Build Premium Value in Your Middle Market Company. This keynote will help leaders understand exactly what drives value in their company and, most importantly, how to go about building a consensus on the steps to take to make their vision a reality.

Developing the Next Generation of Leaders. Developing the next generation of leaders is one of the primary responsibilities of any organization, but 67 percent of companies said they needed to entirely revamp their middle-manager development. This keynote explores the best practices in leadership development and reveals how leadership development depends on practicing, changing, and learning new concepts.

VALUE BUILDING CONSULTING

Marty has facilitated hundreds of board-level meetings and planning sessions for businesses and associations of every size and type. A key feature in each of these facilitated sessions is the strategic Value Building process. Value Building is an intense planning process designed to establish a clear direction and create alignment among the company's leaders. This four-step process will create transformational, strategic initiatives based on your current situation, the market conditions, and your long-range objectives.

EXECUTIVE COACHING AND PEER ADVISORY BOARDS

Marty serves as a principal with The Alternative Board. The Alternative Board's business owner advisory boards provide a safe, confidential environment in which business owners from a variety of industries meet to provide additional perspective and spur new ways of doing business.

For more information on any of these services go to
www.martinoneill.net.

About the Author

Martin O'Neill has the perspective and depth of experience needed to guide leaders. As a business operator, he has run start-ups, middle-market companies, and a large division of a Fortune 50 company. As a consultant, he has facilitated hundreds of meetings and planning sessions with businesses and associations of every size and type. As a speaker, he delivers keynotes and seminars that have been described as passionate, motivating, dynamic, and engaging. As a trainer, Marty, along with his team, created a twelve-course online leadership development program directed toward emerging leaders. As an executive coach, Marty challenges CEOs through his role as a certified coach and facilitator with The Alternative Board. He is also the author of *The Power of an Internal Franchise* and *Building Business Value* and coauthor of *Act Like an Owner*.

Marty began his career as an intelligence analyst for the US Air Force. After completing his degree in computer science at the University of Maryland and learning the nuances of project management at Booz, Allen and Hamilton, he cofounded a technology-based company, led two companies through high-growth phases and subsequent successful acquisitions, and led a business unit for a Fortune 50 company.

As a regional director for Boeing, Marty learned the lessons of change leadership while he was responsible for merging the legacy Conquest business with existing Boeing entities. While positioning Boeing for large system integration efforts, Marty also completed

Boeing's extensive executive development program at the Boeing Leadership Center.

At present, Marty spends his time speaking, consulting, and coaching. To reach a wider audience with his leadership message, Marty and his team created an online version of *Next Generation Leaders*. This program takes middle managers through a twelve-course journey of leadership development.

Marty and his team of coaches at The Alternative Board have become trusted advisors to clients by challenging them to take an honest look at their company, providing them with the tools necessary to build long-term enterprise value, and then holding them accountable to their personal vision.

Marty has a master's of business administration from Loyola College and serves on the boards of several organizations. He loves his involvement with his church's adult faith formation program, remains addicted to watching rugby and playing music in a neighborhood cover band, and continues to reside in Maryland with his wonderful wife and business partner, Denise O'Neill, and their three children, Jack, Liam, and Lily.